Other Books by Lottie Beth Hobbs

Victory Over Trials –
Encouragement from the life of Job

If You Would See Good Days –
Help for daily decisions

Your Best Friend–
The privilege of friendship with Christ

You Can Be Beautiful –
With beauty that never fades

Daughters of Eve –
Strength for today from women of yesterday

2nd printing
Choosing Life's Best
ISBN 0-913838-13-6

Copyright, 1988
Harvest Publications
Fort Worth, Texas

ALL RIGHTS RESERVED. No portion of this book may be reproduced in any form without written permission of the Publisher.

Preface

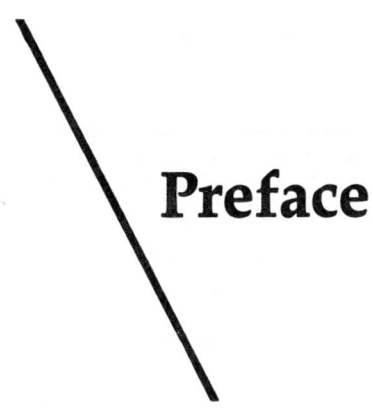

Each day is a treasure unexcelled.

Each day is a precious privilege, for time is limited — few days that pass so swiftly.

Each day of life is a gift from God — God the Giver; man the receiver.

Each day is a sacred trust, a stewardship for which each must account.

Each day is a series of choices. These choices determine our successes and failures now, and our eternal destiny.

In light of these principles, the questions arise: How do we choose life's best? How can we make the most of this precious gift and treasure?

This writer surely claims no special knowledge or insight. However, all of us can go to the God of all wisdom and beseech Him as Solomon did in the long ago:

I am but a little child: I know not how to go out or come in ... give therefore thy servant an understanding heart (I Ki. 3:7-9).

The glorious thought is that it's our choice! We *can know* what constitutes the best life, and we *can choose* to achieve it.

Lottie Beth Hobbs

THIS SERIES IS DESIGNED FOR INDIVIDUAL OR CLASS USE

Numerous Scripture citations are given, perhaps many more than a teacher would deem appropriate for use during a class period. They are given for documentation and for more comprehensive private study. The sections at the close of each chapter are as stated: FOR THOUGHT OR DISCUSSION, supplemental points to be used at the teacher's or reader's discretion.

CONCERNING THE QUOTES of secular proverbs and poems: original source has been given whenever possible to ascertain. However, many are truisms which have developed through the ages — so often repeated that they have become an integral part of many cultures because they are condensed statements of truth. Note how many of the thoughts originated with principles given long ago through Solomon and other sacred writers. Indeed, proverbs — whether sacred or secular — continue to live. The reason is aptly expressed by many writers, such as:

A proverb is the wisdom of years crystallized in the wit of a moment.

All the good sense of the world runs into proverbs.

Proverbs are the echoes of experience.

Proverbs are the jewels of the multitude.

The wisdom of nations lies in their proverbs, which are brief and pithy. — Wm. Penn

A frequent review of proverbs should enter into our reading. — Disraeli

A proverb is much light condensed in one flash. — Simmons

THE CHALLENGE:

*The ideal life, the life of full completion,
haunts us all; we feel the thing we ought
to be beating beneath the thing we are.*

— *Phillip Brooks*

THE SOLUTION:

*Trust in the LORD with all thine heart:
And lean not unto thine own understanding.
In all thy ways acknowledge him,
And he shall direct thy paths.*

— *Proverbs 3:5,6*

Contents

1. The Success Plan That Works / 11
2. A Well-rounded Personality / 21
3. Light for Today / 33
4. How to Be a Hero / 43
5. Honestly! / 55
6. A Precious Jewel / 67
7. A Gracious Woman / 79
8. A Strong Man / 89
9. Precious and Pleasant Riches / 101
10. It Takes a Lot of Courage / 113
11. The Sweetness of a Friend / 125
12. Success in Business / 135
13. A Place of Refuge / 147
14. Today I Will / 159

*In Proverbs, the bud.
In Christ, the blossom.*

1 The Success Plan That Works

Success is on the minds of millions each day. Some merely wish for it. Others consciously strive for it. Countless volumes have been written, and millions spent, in search of the secret of success. Yet it's no secret at all. The formula was given long ago by the Source of Success. It is available for all to see, to possess, and to enjoy.

Throughout the ages thoughtful men and women have sought the highest good. One quality which distinguishes us from animals is the ability to contemplate life's possibilities and to strive toward them. We are not animals, though we may at times fall to a disappointing level. And we are not tumbleweeds on a West Texas prairie, though we are at times tossed about by strong winds. Instead, we are immortal beings with the power of choice and decision. And how far-reaching are those choices!

True success is achieved only by the wise. In fact, success and wisdom are inseparably connected and entwined. Then what is wisdom? How do we incorporate it into our lives? Where do we find the blueprint for so doing? To explore these questions is our purpose.

The Sage of the Ages

"He that walketh with wise men shall be wise" (Prov. 13:20). In ancient Babylon there was a Temple of Learning, open to all for counsel with men of wisdom. A treasured privilege indeed! But it can't compare with our privilege, for we can go to the inexhaustible reservoir of wisdom and "walk with the wise." This includes the *Book of Proverbs*.

Long before the time of secular philosophers such as Socrates, Plato, or Aristotle, a young man named Solomon became king of Israel. He loved the Lord, who said to him in a dream: "Ask what I shall give thee." Solomon requested nothing but wisdom to rule his people well. This pleased God, who promised not only wisdom unexcelled but wealth unequaled (I Ki. 3:5-15).

Critics say it was only a young man's dream, fantasy and not fact. However, other Scriptures specify that "God gave Solomon wisdom and understanding exceeding much, and largeness of heart, even as the sand that is on the seashore ... For he was wiser than all men" (I Ki. 4:29-34). God made him so.

The young king became a wonder of the world: business man, poet, naturalist, political leader, judge, philosopher, military genius, and builder of the world's most magnificent temple. His life surely refutes those who say that a person can be proficient in only one field! Of all Solomon's achievements, however, his writings are most notable. The temple has been destroyed. Other accomplishments have faded. But his words of wisdom have never been equaled. They are as alive, needed, and workable today as ever. Scripture citations used herein are from *Proverbs*, unless otherwise specified.

The Practical Wisdom of *Proverbs*

Every fundamental of abundant living can be found in *Proverbs*. And the plan really works. Why? Solomon penned not merely his own ideas. He was an instrument through whom God gave a workable way of life. Those to whom the oracles of God were committed (Rom. 3:2) have always affirmed Solomon's writings to be inspired. Christ confirmed authenticity when he commended the Queen of Sheba for coming "from the utmost parts of the earth to hear the wisdom of Solomon" (Lk. 11:31). So the pen was Solomon's but the words were inspired by God.

For every blossom in the teachings of Christ, a bud may be found in *Proverbs*. They are inseparable. This is quite understandable, for in Christ "are hid all the treasures of wisdom and knowledge" (Col. 2:3). "Christ, the power of God, and the wisdom of God" (I Cor. 1:24). Since the power and wisdom of God, in all fullness and beauty, are found in Christ, our study will necessarily include Spirit-inspired writings of the New Testament.

Proverbs is as up-to-date as this morning's newspaper — not musty, out-dated rules, a mere relic of a by-gone era. Rather, it strips away all veneer and tells it like it is, reaching into every heart in a remarkably personal way. Readers become amazed that human nature, temptations, sins, and problems are exactly the same today as centuries ago. Practices so prevalent now (thought by some to be new, the "in" thing) are minutely and realistically described, lifted from dens of darkness, bared and spot-lighted, and labeled for what they really are: sin. These powerful pictures, drawn with pinpoint accuracy, should cause the guilty to writhe in shameful discomfort as they recognize themselves all too well in actions they thought to be forever hidden.

Proverbs gives practical solutions. Life is too short to learn everything from experience. One difference between a wise person and a foolish one is the ability to learn from others' mistakes. Every generation has a tendency to think that lessons learned by previous generations do not apply now. Thus, young people often become impatient with their elders' counsel. If your parents or grandparents bequeathed you a million dollars, would you refuse the gift because it was earned by a previous generation? Of course not! A legacy of experience is far more valuable than a legacy of gold. So how foolish to refuse it! The more we can learn from the past, the less pain we pay for our necessary lessons.

Solomon's advice is presented not so much as a preacher on a platform, but more as a technician in a laboratory, clearly showing what will work or fail. Herein lies its practical value. The experiments have already been made for us, the results recorded, enabling us to avoid many deplorable mistakes.

Nothing could be more relevant than the common sense approach of *Proverbs*. There is a tendency today to ridicule the simple virtues: honesty, purity, diligence. Who needs them? Everybody, because they make sense. What if they were eliminated completely? Who would want to live in such a society? Even those who flout and ridicule these values want to live in a world made better by them. They want other people to practice them!

The Uniqueness of *Proverbs*

Proverbs is different from any other book ever written.

The theme is different: "The fear of the Lord is the beginning of wisdom" (1:7; 9:10). When Solomon gave this to the world, it was totally new, a completely different approach to spiritual and intellectual excellence. The theme is enlarged in this all-inclusive statement:

> *Trust in the LORD with all thine heart; and*
> *Lean not unto thine own understanding.*
> *In all thy ways acknowledge him,*
> *And he shall direct thy paths* (3:5,6).

This is the formula for a successful and enriched life. The rest of the Bible, and certainly the whole of our study, amplifies this Scripture. It is the germ, the kernel, the compass, the anchor, the chart, the shield, the sword, and the comforter.

The appeal of Proverbs is different. When a person is told that something is *sinful,* he is likely to be reluctant to give it up. However, when the action is described as *stupid,* he is more inclined to let it go. This is the basis of Solomon's appeal. More than anyone before or since, he emphasized sin's folly. A continuous thread through the entire book is: "It's smart to be good. It's foolish to do otherwise, so don't be stupid! Be good to yourself by doing right" (8:35,36).

The style of Proverbs is different. Every chord of the heart is touched: an appeal to honor, reverence, piety, love, fear, self-respect, intelligence, and self-interest. To accomplish this, varying methods are employed: vivid description, contrast, and repetition.

Vivid descriptions of some common sins are found only in *Proverbs.* The New Testament teaches that drunkenness will destroy the soul, but only *Proverbs* pictures realistically how alcohol affects the body and spirit. It's an accurate, up-to-date portrayal unexcelled in secular literature. Only *Proverbs* lucidly describes a designing woman who weaves her destructive web around an unsuspecting young man. Only *Proverbs* graphically portrays the pathetic existence of a lazy person.

Contrast is frequently used: good vs. evil; wisdom vs. folly; reward vs. punishment. Approaching sins from different angles, in effect Wisdom says to us: "Look at the other side of the coin. Suppose you don't choose to do right. What then? Look at your alternative."

The way of transgressors is hard (13:15).

Repetition adds weight. One method of teaching used by oriental parents was the frequent repetition of pithy, concise statements of truth. Repetition is used throughout *Proverbs*; thus, we shall explore the book by subjects, not verse by verse.

Concise, energetic, penetrating statements lend force to the book. "Proverb" is from two root words: "pro" meaning "for," and "verb" meaning "word." A proverb is a word or short statement taking the place of a lengthy discourse — hence, a sentence sermon. A proverb is condensed wisdom, a valuable sign-post on life's road.

For Whom Is *Proverbs* Written?

It is for everyone. No person can read the book without profit.

For young people. Those who absorb the wisdom of *Proverbs* will be far wiser than older people who refuse to do so. It is a priceless guide, a sure anchor in life's storms. It is a blueprint for developing admirable men and women who are a joy to their parents, a blessing to others, and an honor to their Creator. If you want to be super-smart, to master the art of living, then master *Proverbs*. It is truly an education within itself. Just think what an enlightened understanding of *Proverbs* could do — for this generation and all that follow.

> *My son, keep thy father's commandment, and forsake not the law of thy mother: Bind them continually upon thine heart, and tie them about thy neck. When thou goest,* it shall *lead* thee; *and when thou sleepest,* it shall *keep* thee; *and when thou awakest,* it shall *talk* with thee. *For the commandment is a lamp; and the law is light; and reproofs of instruction are the way of life* (6:20-23).

For those who are older. No matter how spiritually mature one may become, life continues to bring new perplexities.

Proverbs furnishes an approach which may have been overlooked, practical answers not found elsewhere in sacred or secular writings. The preface states the purpose:

> *To give subtilty to the simple, to the young man knowledge and discretion. A wise man will hear and will increase learning (1:4,5).*

For men the book presents a standard which will make a man admirably strong in all relationships — whether business man, king, servant, husband, father, or friend.

> *A wise man is strong (24:5).*

For women it is a jewel unexcelled. It warns against everything a woman should not be, describing one who lives in the depths of degradation, pulling down all she touches. Then in a picturesque climax, the book portrays the highest possibilities of noble womanhood — an elevating, encouraging influence wherever she goes. And a mother who follows it will experience such joy, for her children "arise up and call her blessed."

> *Her price is far above rubies . . . let her own works praise her (31:10,31).*

For parents. Truths clothed in concise and vivid language can become a part of a child's thinking forever. Oft-repeated gems stick indelibly in the memory, ever ready to help in times of critical decisions. A widow who reared four Christian sons was asked: "How did you do it?" She replied: "When we faced problems, we often read *Proverbs* together." This blends parental tenderness with divine authority. What a lifetime blessing for any child! One prominent pioneer preacher required all his children to memorize the entire book of *Proverbs*.

Train up a child in the way he should go: and when he is old, he will not depart from it (22:6).

For these reasons, it is highly profitable for everyone to read one chapter each day in *Proverbs*, corresponding with the day of the month, completing the 31 chapters each month. This can stamp our minds indelibly with God-ordained and time-tested truths needed every day throughout life.

Principles to Ponder

Some important principles shine throughout the writings of Solomon:

Success is possible. It is encouraging to realize that true success is possible for anyone. There is no limited amount of it. Nobody has a corner on the market.

There is enough success to go around
For all who help themselves.

Success is personal. Parents may bequeath children material possessions, a good name, and a worthy example. They may teach about abundant living, but each person must achieve it for himself. Our conduct brings consequences which are ours alone, whether good or evil, wise or foolish. "If thou be wise, thou shalt be wise for thyself: but if thou scornest, thou alone shall bear it" (9:12).

We may stand for awhile in the reflected glory of others' accomplishments; but sooner or later we must face our Judge, the most personal experience imaginable. No one can do this for us. "So then every one of us shall give account of himself to God" (Rom. 14:12). Then each person stands or falls, fails or succeeds.

Success must be purposeful. It cannot be achieved accidentally. People know the necessity of definite planning for an education, a vocation, a vacation, the skill of playing golf or the piano; but many have no idea how to plan for achievement in life's most profound and enduring aspects. So they drift through life wondering why they feel restless and lacking in meaningful accomplishments. Those who fail to plan, plan to fail.

No person is born great or has greatness thrust upon him. It is an achievement found in *being*, not in *having*, — in being somebody; and the more anyone becomes like God, the greater he or she becomes.

So each person can choose life's best. It is for "whosoever will" — a deliberate act of the will followed by a calculated course of action. Nothing is more prominently taught by Inspiration, and confirmed by observation.

FOR THOUGHT OR DISCUSSION

- *Proverbs* is the world's masterpiece on wisdom. Yet, many view this word as a vague academic and abstract term difficult to translate into everyday life. So what is wisdom? First, it is a Personality, for God is the primary Source. "He giveth wisdom unto the wise, and knowledge to them that know nothing" (Dan. 2:20). In *Proverbs* wisdom is movingly personified, portraying the eternal existence, incomparable worth, and the absolute necessity of following the Voice which cries out to all (8:1-36). Later Revelation reveals that Christ embodied wisdom (Col. 2:3; I Cor. 1:24). "Let the word of Christ dwell in you richly in all wisdom" (Col. 3:16).

    Just as every road in England leads finally to London, so every Scripture leads finally to Christ. Anyone who fails to trace this golden thread of truth explores the Word without the necessary Key. Surely neither Solomon nor his contemporaries realized this fuller meaning, bearing testimony that he wrote by guidance of the Holy Spirit (II Pet. 1:21).

- Does knowledge constitute wisdom? What is the difference? Knowledge is an essential part of wisdom, and the words are at times used interchangeably. Yet there is a difference. Knowledge is the foundation; wisdom is the entire structure, proper use of knowledge. One may be able to quote the entire Bible and still lack wisdom, if he fails to incorporate its teachings into his life. James admonishes us to pray for wisdom — NOT knowledge (Jas. 1:5). We study the Word for knowledge. Fear of God motivates us to increase wisdom through prayer and incorporating the Scriptures into our lives (II Tim. 3:14,15). This enables us to become Wisdom reflected, as the moon reflects the sun.

- More than any other writer, Solomon contrasts wisdom and folly. Who is a fool? The Hebrew word for "fool" is a strong word, meaning "crass, stupid, insensible.' Since folly is diametrically opposed to wisdom, anyone who fails to follow the Words of Wisdom classifies himself as a foolish person. Learning to identify and avoid foolish conduct is a lifetime task and challenge, confirming the tremendous value of Solomon's judicious admonitions.

BRIEF OUTLINE OF PROVERBS

I. THE PURPOSE OF THE BOOK (1:1-6).

II. THE WORTH OF WISDOM (1 - 9). How valuable (3:13-18).

III. INDIVIDUAL PRACTICAL PROVERBS (10 - 22:16). 374 proverbs in couplets, probably nucleus of whole book.

IV. "THE WORDS OF THE WISE" (22:17 - 24:34). Another collection of proverbs. Changes form of verse, quatrain used mostly.

V. PROVERBS ARRANGED BY THE MEN OF HEZEKIAH (25 - 29). Evidently proverbs of Solomon copied out during time of Hezekiah.

VI. THE WORDS OF AGUR AND LEMUEL (30 - 31). No information concerning them. Strong belief that King Lemuel might have been just a name taken by Solomon.

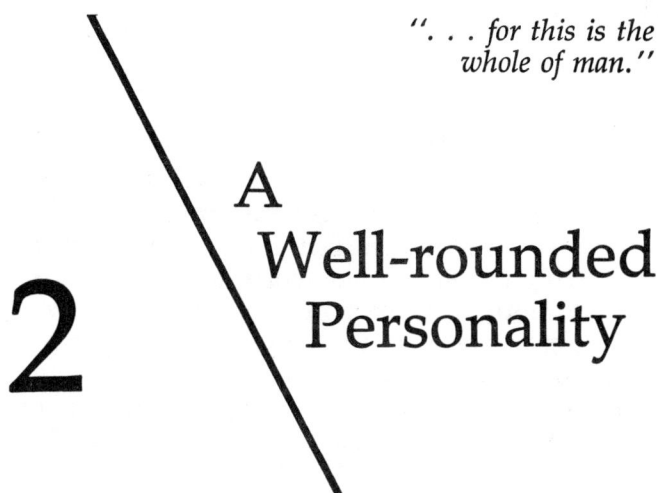

". . . for this is the whole of man."

2   A Well-rounded Personality

Several years ago in a symposium for psychiatrists in Dallas, Texas, a noted psychiatrist dealt with developing the "whole person." He concluded: "A feeling of whole-ism is necessary, and this is not possible if one rejects God."

Much has been said about the "whole person," the "well-rounded personality," the "fulfilled life." This is not new. Solomon, in his writings from beginning to end, defines not only what the fulfilled life *is* but what it *is not*. Through inspiration and a lifetime of trial-and-error experience, the aging Solomon summed it up: "Fear God and keep his commandments, for this is the whole duty of man" (Eccl. 12:13). The word "duty" was added by the translators. The original Hebrew says: "This is the whole of man."

Clearly the Sage of the Ages is saying: "This is the way to be a whole person, to have a fulfilled life, a well-rounded personality." How? "Fear God and keep his commandments." A six-word formula. Simple, isn't it? So simple that secular philosophers scoff at it. So simple that most people overlook it in their frantic pursuit of an elusive "something."

Who Is a Whole Person?

Success with self is essential. The world's applause is but a vain and hollow echo in an empty heart, if one has no respect for the person he sees in the mirror each day. Abundant living requires inner worth and integrity, or else we live constantly with someone we actually despise. We could sail the seas, rocket to the moon or Mars; but when we arrived, we would find the one person from which there is no escape — ourselves. But this is not the end of the matter. We must also live with ourselves in eternity. Death does not transform us. It merely transports us.

How essential then to develop a self fit to live with! A difficult and important challenge — to conquer, to train, to ennoble ourselves — a self-mastery achieved through self-discipline, not self-indulgence.

Success with others is also necessary. No person is an island. To enjoy the respect and favor of associates is a critical need: home relationships, business relationships, and other friendships.

Meeting this challenge is not easy. A survey of employers revealed that the major cause of employee dismissal is the inability to get along with others. The escalating divorce rate also confirms the gravity of this problem. But "favor and good understanding in the sight of God and man" (3:4) is an attainable goal: an honorable reputation, a good name, which is "rather to be chosen than great riches, and loving favor rather than silver and gold" (22:1) and a life remembered by others with joy (10:7). Of all God's creatures, only man can enjoy the esteem of his fellows. However, even this does not provide the longed-for "whole-ness."

Success with God is the hub of the wheel for the well-rounded, smooth-running life. What would happen to the wheel of an auto or a wagon, if the hub should be removed? or improperly placed? It would completely break down, its usefulness destroyed.

Even secular psychologists stress the importance of "centering" life, emphasizing that a failure to do so causes frustration and unhappiness. However, most secular counselors maintain that the *process* of centering is more vital than the *object* on which life is centered. God's spokesmen have always clearly specified the necessary *object* (Deut. 6:5; Matt. 22:35-37) and Solomon's wisdom implores: *"Trust in the Lord with all thine heart"* (3:5). The *process* alone is powerless in the long run. The *object* of the "centered" life is all-important. Then all other aspects of life fall into proper perspective, forming the longed-for "whole-ness." So God must be not only FIRST on our list, but HE IS the list! "For in him we live, and move, and have our being" (Acts 17:28).

The Most Magnetic Power

If you should go into a plant which manufactures compasses, you would see the needles in the incomplete ones in disarray, going in all directions. However, after the magnet is applied, the compass may be jostled even in turbulent storms and the needle will consistently return to a northward position. Being magnetized, it is stabilized, made useful and dependable, fulfilling its intended purpose.

This is our need. By what power can our lives be magnetized, made useful and dependable, fulfilling our highest potential? In an enlightening, intriguing, and stirring appeal to His wayward children, our Heavenly Father said: "Yea, I have loved thee with an everlasting love: therefore with loving-kindness have I drawn thee" (Jer. 31:3). This identifies the most powerful of all magnets! The Father's loving-kindness.

The entire Bible is a love story, the Father's love for his creation. Not the Hollywood-fabricated counterfeit, but sacrificial concern which regards another's best interest as paramount. This is the essence of our Heavenly Father (I Jno. 4:8). Nothing is even remotely comparable to the magnetic power of the Creator of the Universe, the Power by which the successful life is centered and stabilized. Yet, most people have lost sight of God's greatness and power.

The Eccentric Life

The word "eccentric" means "off center." What happens to a life which has a missing or misplaced "hub" — a center on something or someone other than God? It will eventually break down, a fact established not only by Revelation but by observation and experience.

The most common "hub" is named "Self," though manifested in various ways — a life centered on possessions, pleasure, power, prominence, popularity, profession, peer approval, or family relationships. In recent years there has been an over-abundance of books on self-help, self-esteem, self-improvement, self-image. However, most of the writers reject the Creator and seek to promote a good self-image without Him. They propose simply: "Love yourself. Feel good about yourself. Believe in yourself." These concepts, devoid of eternal spiritual values and responsibilities, created the "Me" generation, according to Dr. Paul C. Vitz, psychologist at New York University, in his excellent book, *Psychology As Religion: The Cult of Self-worship.* Self-worship is inevitable when people are taught to center life around self.

Almighty God or Almighty Man?

Popular philosophies which dethrone the Creator and enthrone man in His place have mushroomed. Two major theories, with various shades of thought, permeate every sector of our society. In principle, their theme song is: "How Great I Art."

- Atheism is appealingly re-labeled Humanism, which openly maintains: "We find insufficient evidence for belief in the existence of a supernatural ... As non-theists, we begin with humans not God, with nature not deity" (*Humanist Manifesto II*, p. 16). All who reject the Creator are forced to embrace the premise that we are nothing more than the product of blind evolutionary chance, a "naked ape." This philosophy doesn't work! No person will strive for pure and lofty living if he believes he is to die like a dog. No person can feel fulfilled and worthwhile if all he can look forward to is a dusty grave and oblivion. Atheism (by whatever name called) is a parasitic system which sucks the life-blood from an individual and leaves him spiritually and emotionally anemic. The result is an insipid, disappointing existence lacking any lasting or far-reaching purpose. Several decades of this bankrupt and hope-destroying theory led many to seek something more meaningful — a spiritual dimension to life.

- However, rather than turning to the spiritual truths of our Creator, some seekers turned to Eastern mystic religions. The result is a Westernized version of mysticism which its advocates call the New Age. They reject Jehovah the Creator, maintaining that "god" IS ALL THINGS: the universe, plants, animals, human beings, concluding therefore that each person IS GOD! This ego-boosting affirmation is growing in popularity, led by well-known people such as the actress who teaches seminar participants to chant repeatedly: "I am god. I am god." Another basic New Age teaching is reincarnation, borrowed from the paganism of Eastern mysticism. It appeals to man's desire to live again, supplanting the annihilation of atheism.

- NOTE that Humanism and New Age-ism both center all things on MAN, while rejecting a CREATOR. Yet, their advocates continually refer to "god." Be aware! They do not mean God, the Creator. This explanation is necessary, for we must understand that the successful life is centered around the omnipotent and omniscient Jehovah portrayed in the Bible — not just anybody or anything which someone may choose to call "god." This center on SELF, this misplaced "hub," is developing a nation of "eccentrics" who live off center!

The Formula for Self-esteem

Self-esteem, like happiness, usually eludes the person who seeks it directly. Why? Both are by-products accruing from basically-engrained concepts. No doubt you have heard counselors affirm that low self-esteem is a major psychological problem. Have you wondered why this problem seems to have escalated in our "enlightened" nation? Think! On every hand — schools, television, literature, and even some churches — people are taught that they are nothing more than an overgrown amoeba, evolved into a two-legged animal, who must stumble through a tumultuous world to an uncertain end. Trying to overcome the resulting feeling of worthlessness by telling a person that he is "god" doesn't solve the problem, for in quieter reflection everyone knows he is inadequate within himself to overcome the burdens and uncontrollable circumstances of life.

On the other hand, think of the feeling of worth engrained in the child who learns from an early age that God made him in His own image, that God is aware of every detail of our lives even before we were born (Psa. 139:14-16), that He cares for the righteous (10:3) and hears their prayers (15:8). Nothing is too small to merit His attention. He knows our name, and the number of hairs on our head. He is aware of every thought, gesture, look, word, mood, and attitude, watching our often-faltering steps with loving-kindness.

Our Creator Father loved us enough to send His Son to earth to show us how to live and how to die. He is preparing an eternal home for His faithful followers. Only great love prompts intense interest in everything another does. The minute by minute activities of mere acquaintances do not absorb your mind. But if you love someone deeply, your interest in that one's thoughts, feelings, and activities is constant, even in absence. So we know God loves us. He cares! Intensely! This shines throughout His Word, including *Proverbs*.

Understanding these principles provides children and adults a sense of self-worth far superior to anything any humanistic psychologist can offer. It is not only useless but destructive to tell a child "Love yourself; feel good about yourself" — unless he is given a firm and effective foundation upon which to build self-worth. Yet secular psychologists totally reject this basic principle. A preacher once sent his son to a psychologist for help. What was the analysis? That the son was fine, that it was the father who needed help because be believed in God and in the Bible as the Word of God.

Failure in Glamorous Living Color

The life of Solomon furnishes, in glamorous living color, a demonstration of what success *is* and *is not*. What does it teach us?

Is success measured by possessions? Today's society seems mesmerized by materialism. The popular attitude is: if you can't wear it, eat it, drive it, bank it, or impress your neighbors with it, it isn't worth very much. One of humanity's tragedies is the tendency to evaluate achievement by externals rather than by inner worth. Possessions and people can so easily produce a false sense of security and importance.

Think a minute. Suppose you should lose your family, friends, job, house, car, and bank account. What would remain? YOU! — and nothing more — the real YOU by which success or failure must be measured. So material wealth is not synonymous with success. It only measures what a person *has*, not what he *is*. Millionaires who take their own lives have everything to live *on*, but find nothing to live *for*.

Does prominence measure success? A high school teacher asked: "How do you define success?" One girl said: "A person known all over the world is successful." Was she right? Think of Hitler, Mussolini, and myriads of others. World prominent but not successful!

Caesar conquered 800 cities and a million foes, but was stabbed to death by his best friends. Napoleon died in banishment, a conquered captive. Judas is world-renowned. He made his mark on history. But was he a success? He desecrated his divinely-given life and opportunity. Christ said it would have been better if he had never been born (Matt. 26:24). What a serious indictment! What a sad commentary!

So worldly acclaim is not synonymous with success — whether political leader, actress, rock star, author, philosopher, or any other prominent person. Names of the world's truly great people are not necessarily found in *Who's Who*, for this is merely an appraisal of how some people view other people.

Does pleasure constitute the good life? Many today equate success with happiness, and equate happiness with physical pleasure. The prevailing idea is: "It's a Playboy World." Our sex-saturated society advocates: "Do your own thing. Ignore all inhibitions. Then indescribable joy will be yours."

This is not new. Solomon was the original Playboy. He tried everything: prominence, power, possessions, silver and gold unequaled, luxurious houses, wine, women, and song. He indulged himself in "any joy," "whatsoever mine eyes desired" (Eccl. 2:10,11). He really lived it up! No doubt he was envied by all his peers.

What was Solomon's appraisal of his own life? Happiness? The fulfilled life? Far from it! He said it was "vanity and vexation of spirit." NOTHING! A troubled, shallow, disappointing way to live. Many today echo Solomon's conclusions. Experience has taught them that searching for life's "highs" in wealth, social-ladder-climbing, promiscuous living, a needle, a bottle, or a pill, is nothing more than tragic disillusionment. The world's pick-me-ups always lead to a crash.

In his personal life Solomon fell far short of perfection, failing to practice the principles he knew; but *his sad and sinful life adds weight to his admonitions.* He has been over the road. He learned from experience, as well as revelation: "The way of transgressors is hard" (13:15). So he beseeches: "Don't try it. It won't work. You will bring agony and destruction on yourself." The self-defeat and slow suicide of sin is a central thought of the Bible, especially emphasized by Solomon.

Logical Conclusions

Wealth, fame, popularity, prominence, sensual pleasure — all bring but temporary satisfaction. Why? Because of their very nature. All are inherently incapable of satisfying the heart's supreme needs. It would be like trying to sustain the body with sawdust. Sawdust is good, not evil, but it simply does not have the inherent power to sustain life. To expect such would be assigning it an impossible role.

So it is with all material and fleshly aspects of life, which are good and God-ordained when properly used; but to expect them to nourish our spirit and fill the inner void is expecting the impossible. To center life around a temporary tabernacle soon destined for the grave — to adorn it, to pamper it, to exalt it, to indulge it — while neglecting the eternal spirit within, is indeed not the smart way to go. This is the message Solomon implores us to learn.

No wonder he teaches: "The fear of the Lord is the beginning of knowledge" (1:7). Everything has a beginning, and the first step toward the abundant and successful life is "the fear of the Lord." What does this mean? A reverential respect — reverence for His divine nature and His complete authority. Without it, there is no excellence for which to strive. Without it, no person even tries to live right. One who fears not God spurns no evil. He has no such interest or incentive, but follows his own selfish desires. However, "by the fear of the Lord, men depart from evil" (16:6). "The fear of the Lord is a fountain of life to depart from the snares of death" (14:27). "Fountain of life" — refreshing, life-sustaining, satisfying.

Eccl. 12:13

"Fear God and *keep his commandments.*" This provides our direction for this incredible journey called *life.* With God at the center, all other relationships, all problems, all joys, all accomplishments, all goals, fall into proper perspective.

FOR THOUGHT OR DISCUSSION

- Reincarnation is not a "new and enlightened" doctrine. Rather, it is retrogression to the paganism of Hinduism. Then what is its appeal in a supposedly enlightened and civilized society? (Surveys show that approximately one-fourth of all Americans believe in it.) The teaching is "If you don't get it right this time, you simply try again when you come back." This offers a longed-for *hope* of life after death, while *obliterating the concept of guilt and sin and accountability to a Supreme Being.* Many find this extremely comforting. But is it true? Only one Scripture is needed to totally refute this false pagan doctrine: "It is appointed unto men ONCE to die, but AFTER THIS THE JUDGMENT" (Heb. 9:27) — NOT another life on earth!

- Is it wrong to use the fear of God to persuade people to do right? Read II Cor. 5:11 and Heb. 10:31; 12:29.

- Is success dependent upon one's spouse? Surely a happy marriage is one of life's cherished attainments and joys, but giant footprints on the sands of time have been made by men and women without the aid and encouragement of a companion. All records show that Abraham Lincoln's marriage was surely not ideal. All his achievements were in spite of a selfish and vexatious wife. Surely that was not easy, but it proves that such unhappy circumstances do not spell failure. Or, indeed, is success dependent on marriage at all? The apostle Paul, talented and intellectual, was not married. Yet, without a doubt, he remains through the centuries one of the world's brightest luminaries.

- Who is the best husband? the best wife? One who loves God above all, for then he/she goes to God for direction in building a happy marriage. Could anyone wish for a better companion? Who is the best employer? employee? friend? One whose love for God is paramount. That person is careful to treat others with thoughtfulness and kindness, as the Father instructs.

- Each person is either a blot or a blessing in the world — never a blank. By learning to succeed as a friend, neighbor, family member, employee, employer, or leader in any field, we bless not only ourselves but enrich all society. It's a NO-FAIL PLAN for everyone concerned.

Quotes to Consider

He who builds according to every man's advice will have a crooked house. — Danish proverb

It is less painful to learn in youth than to be ignorant in age.

A life without a purpose is a ship without a rudder.

Live to do good and you will never tire of your employment.

Good counsel is no better than bad counsel, if it be not taken in time.

A danger foreseen is half avoided.

What is the use of running if we are not on the right road? — German proverb

Man carries his superiority inside, animals theirs outside.

He who provides for this life, but takes no care for eternity, is wise for a moment, but a fool for eternity. — Tillotson

Liberty cannot be established without morality, nor morality without faith. — Horace Greeley

A little philosophy inclineth a man's mind to atheism; but depth in philosophy bringeth man's minds about to religion. — Bacon

From a pure source pure water comes. — Latin proverb

The day is long and the day is hard;
We are tired of the march and of keeping guard;
Tired of the sense of a fight to be won,
Of days to live through, and of work to be done;
Tired of ourselves and of being alone.

And all the while, did we only see,
We walk in the Lord's own company;
We fight, but 'tis he who nerves our arm;
He turns the arrows which else might harm,
And out of the storm he brings a calm.

—Susan Coolidge

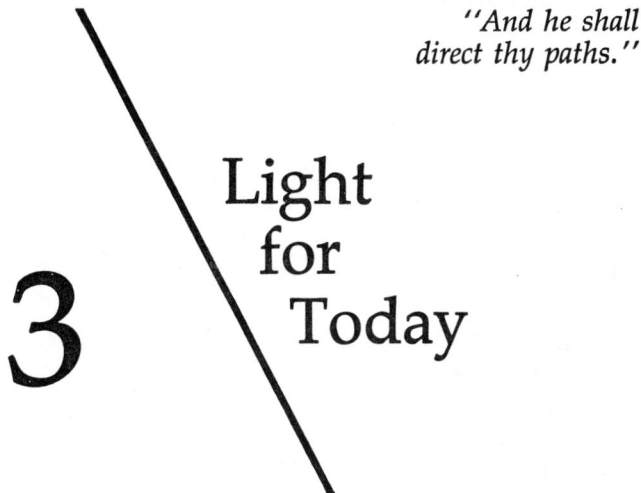

"And he shall direct thy paths."

3 Light for Today

A biologist once made an experiment. He constructed a box with a suspended center-piece covered with soil and planted with seeds. He made a hole in the top and placed the box in the sunlight. Soon plants appeared, sticking their heads through the hole. He then closed the top hole and made a hole in the bottom of the box. Before long, the plants appeared through the bottom opening. Then the bottom hole was closed. After a time, he opened the box and found a tangled mass of plants. With no light, they had no sense of direction. The result was complete confusion and eventual death. No doubt you have many times watched plants reach for the sunlight.

Yes, light is necessary for life and direction. So it is in the spiritual realm. Without light, life becomes tangled chaos. Every minute of every day, we need light and a sense of direction. Where do we find it?

There are only two possible sources: (1) human intellect or feelings, or (2) a Power greater than, and separate from, human beings. Which is valid? On which can we rely?

"Lean Not to Thine Own Understanding"

Just as the tangled, confused roots could not get light from a "fellow root" or reach within themselves for light, so it is with us. *Light must come from an outside source:* "It is not within man that walketh to direct his own steps" (Jer. 10:23). Yet, many continue to try.

One of today's most popular teachings is that each person can find "within self" the necessary guidance, the answers to life's questions. This is sold to the public under many different guises. Whether labeled psychology, religion, or education, the ultimate result is the same: a chaotic life which breaks down. Why is this true?

The Limitations of Human Intelligence

This man-on-his-own, pull-yourself-up-by-your-own-bootstraps philosophy is not new. The Greeks tried it. They rejected God and sought wisdom from within themselves (I Cor. 1:18-31). The Romans tried it. The tragic and destructive results are recorded (Rom. 1:21-23). Every person who rejects the Creator becomes his own god, his own guide, sailing on turbulent seas without chart or compass. Why are human beings incapable of directing themselves?

Man is a transcient earth-creature, living as a vapor on a planet he did not create and cannot control. It is the height of egotism and folly to boast of self-sufficiency. Robert Ingersoll, prominent infidel, speaking at his brother's funeral, said: "Every cradle says 'Whence?' and every coffin says 'Whither?' " He admitted ignorance, the questioning, but never found the answers. Of course not! Man is totally incapable of finding the answers through his own knowledge. Human ignorance is sharply contrasted with Omniscience in Proverbs 30:2-4.

The fickleness of all human thinking proves our inability to direct ourselves. Man's mind fluctuates. It seethes with thoughts that are alternately certain and uncertain, selfish and unselfish, sinful and good. How often have you experienced this? At one moment things may seem clearly to be one way. Then in minutes, or days, or years, the same things seem altogether different. This is true of all human thinking, confirmed by the vacillating conclusions of some of the world's most astute minds. All who live by man's philosophy, no matter how seemingly brilliant, can never rise any higher than the philosopher, and can never be sure of *anything*.

Man's helplessness proves the folly of relying on human intelligence. In the presence of natural disasters — floods, earthquakes, hurricanes, tornadoes, or death — who can be egotistical enough to boast of self-sufficiency?

Technology (science) is insufficient. One prominent atheist sadly and reluctantly observed: "Man can go to the moon, but he still acts like a quarrelsome ape." It will always be so, unless people follow a Guide greater than human intelligence.

Scientific technology is not the answer, no matter how sophisticated. The magnificent space achievements were made possible by the discovery and use of natural laws. Who made these laws? Who made the universe and kept it running with split-second precision for centuries before the scientists' discoveries? Human beings can only *discover* and *utilize*, being absolutely powerless to *create* anything, or to *change natural laws*.

Therefore, man on his own is ignorant, fickle, helpless, and insufficient. All this confirms the futility and folly of leaning on our own understanding. Of course, any person who rejects the Creator is forced to lean on human ignorance and frailty. Such a weak crutch! Such a sad choice!

The Folly of Leaning on Feelings

A popular doctrine has blossomed in the 20th century. Its

advocates reject or minimize both reason (the intellect) and the infallibility of Scripture, and then base all "answers" on an irrational "leap of faith," a subjective and non-communicable experience which affirms: "I just *feel* that God wants me to do this or that." Though its leaders claim to be within the fold of Christianity, the very premise is false and anti-Christian. Intuition, subjective feelings, a blind "leap of faith" were possible before Christ came. If these are capable of guiding us and reconciling us to our Maker, then Christ's death was altogether unnecessary and cruel. A blasphemous indictment against God!

Feelings (emotions) are misleading, unreliable, unstable, and at times uncontrollable — affected by such trivial things as the weather, our health, the mood of those around us, the success or failure of an attempted project or treasured relationship.

Feelings are powerless to teach truth, or what we *should believe*. They reflect only what we *do believe*, which may be false. For example, some heathen women sacrifice their babies to the Nile River and then *feel* blessed, righteous, contented. Their feelings do not affirm or constitute truth but merely reflect their false beliefs, producing wrong conduct.

Suppose you received a telegram: "Your son has been killed." How would you *feel*? Suppose, however, you later received news that you son was *not dead*, but indeed alive. Your *feelings* would change quickly. Your initial grief was not based on *truth*, but on error which you *believed to be truth*.

Therefore, *"I think" or "I feel" (my "hunches" or intellectual conclusions) can never be a reliable guide or an accurate indication of the Lord's will.* We must consciously educate and train our intellect by God's word, bringing our will into harmony with God's will. Then our emotions will fall into proper place.

Self-delusion is so dangerous and prevalent that we are warned of it again and again. "Tapping inner power" is not enough. Our inner power must be plugged into the Source of Power — or lives can be as ineffective as an unplugged electrical appliance, in spite of tremendous potential.

> *There is a way that seemeth right unto a man; but the end thereof are the ways of death (16:25).*
>
> *Every way of a man is right in his own eyes: but the Lord pondereth the hearts (21:2).*
>
> *Lean not unto thine own understanding (3:5).*

The Necessary Light

Nothing is more surely taught, or more easily observed, than the fact that we are incapable of directing ourselves. It's useless and foolish to try. Then how can we keep our lives from becoming tangled chaos — as the tangled roots deprived of light? Where do we find the necessary light?

God is the primary source. "God is light, and in him is no darkness at all" (I Jno. 1:5). "There are many devices in a man's heart; nevertheless, the counsel of the Lord, that shall stand" (19:21). The only sure and dependable counsel comes from the Lord.

Only through His Word can we know this counsel and appropriate the essential light to our lives. "The entrance of thy words giveth light" (Psa. 119:130). "For the commandment is a lamp: and the law is light" (6:23). "Thy word is a lamp unto my feet, and a light unto my path" (Psa. 119:105).

Christ is the incarnation and demonstration of Light, in word and deeds. "I am the light of the world: he that followeth me shall not walk in darkness, but shall have the light of life" (Jno. 8:12). "The Word was made flesh, and dwelt among us." Read of this glorious embodiment of Light in John 1:1-18. The Son portrays the Sun of righteousness for all the world to see.

Christ's followers reflect this Light, as the moon reflects the sun. This is a commandment (Matt. 5:14-16) — but think of the exalted privilege! In a world filled with darkness and pain, we have not only the responsibility but the privilege of shining in this darkness, reflecting the glorious light of Christ and our Heavenly Father — every minute, every day, in all circumstances. It is not possible to choose a life any more exalted or fulfilling, or more needed by the world. What a self-esteem builder! One which the disbeliever denies himself.

"In All Thy Ways"

"In all thy ways acknowledge him, and he shall direct thy paths" (3:6). The promise is conditional. God directs the paths of *those who acknowledge him in all their ways.* What does this mean? To acknowledge not only His existence but His authority to instruct us in *all our ways,* in everything we do and say. To summarize principles discussed more fully later, let's ask ourselves: do we go to Him for authority and instructions?

In ways of attitude and disposition?
In ways of entertainment and recreation?
In ways of caring for our physical body?
In ways of dealing with associates?
In ways of making a living?
In ways of moral conduct?
In ways of worship?
In ways of speech?
In ways of influence?
In ways of home life?

Living, Active, Powerful

"He shall direct thy paths." He does so through His written Word, which some mistakenly believe to be only musty

history and out-dated rules with little relationship to minute by minute, hour by hour living. Far, far from it!

For the word of God is quick [living] and powerful, and sharper than any two-edged sword, piercing even to the dividing asunder of soul and spirit, and of the joints and marrow, and is a discerner of the thoughts and intents of the heart (Heb. 4:12).

Nothing is more powerful than words, whether spoken or written. Why? Words are the essence of the spirit, or mind — non-material vehicles by which ideas are carried from one heart (spirit) to another. Then the ultimate power is the Word of the Creator of the Universe. And this Word is *living* and *more powerful than any sword.* All who speak of the Bible as a "dead letter" merely reveal their misinformation. Jesus, sent by the Father as the Sun of righteousness (Mal. 4:2) said:

It is the spirit that quickeneth [makes alive] . . . the words that I speak unto you, they are spirit, and they are life (Jno. 6:63).

Words which are "spirit and life." Words just as alive and effective today as when first spoken. Without the written Word we can know absolutely nothing of what the Father and the Son have done for us, or what they ask us to do.

Indeed, God's Word is the only foundation for a sure and valid faith, for "faith cometh by hearing, and hearing by the word of God" (Rom. 10:17). Faith is not plucked out of the air or built in the imagination!

The power of God's word is specified in hundreds of Scriptures. By his Word all things were formed (Heb. 11:3) and are upheld (Heb. 1:3). His Word is the incorruptible seed which makes our spiritual re-birth possible, and it will live forever (I Pet. 1:23-25). By the Word we will be judged (Rev. 20;12; Jno. 12:48). Only two things will outlive this world and exist in eternity: the Word of God and the soul of man.

So to bring our souls into harmony with the Word is life's real purpose.

An amazing and enlightening Scripture is the 119th Psalm. Do yourself a favor. Read all 176 verses. With the exception of about five verses, every verse in the Psalm deals with the Word: its power, authority, and effectiveness. The Word is truth (v. 142) and righteousness (v. 172). It restrains us from evil (v. 9-11, 59), gives hope and comfort (v. 49,50), gives understanding (v. 130) and can make us wiser than the world's teachers, ancient or modern (98-100). The Word provides songs in the night (or troubles) of life (v. 54,55). It is dependable, unchangeable, eternal: "For ever, O Lord, thy word is settled in heaven" (v. 89).

The Best Buy in the World

"Buy the truth and sell it not" (23:23). How and where do we *buy* truth? Not in a supermarket — not even in the "supermarket of ideas" as some claim. To enjoy the world's best buy, we must learn to recognize it.

To determine the nature of truth is the most fundamental of all decisions. From this one point stems every religious controversy. Is truth knowable, fixed, unchangeable? Or is it relative, vacillating, changing from time to time, from person to person? It can't be both, for these two concepts are contradictory and mutually exclusive. We must decide, and upon our decision rests our spiritual destiny.

In every field (astronomy, mathematics, history, etc.) truth is fixed, knowable, and unchangeable.

Ten people seeing an accident may have ten contradictory versions. But the *truth* is: it happened *only one way*, not ten. The investigator interviews all ten, searching for truth — unchangeable truth which exists whether the officer ever finds it or not.

You were born a specific year, day, minute. That truth

will never change, no matter what anyone may wish or say.

H_2O constituted water long before human beings discovered this fact. 2 plus 2 equaled four before anyone so declared it.

So in every field, we search — not because *truth* is lost, but because *we are!* Truth does not vary with society's appraisal, opinions, wishes, or failure to search.

Does this principle apply in spiritual matters? It is totally unreasonable to think the Creator would institute knowable and dependable laws of science, gravity, mathematics, etc., and then leave us with no dependable and absolute law in the most crucial aspect of life, the spiritual.

- *Truth is God's Word.* Christ said to the Father: "Thy word is truth" (Jno. 17:17). So Truth is synonomous with Light. Both are manifested through the Word.
- *Truth is knowable and understandable.* "Ye shall know the truth, and the truth shall make you free" (Jno. 8:32). If truth is not fixed and knowable, then no person can enjoy the promised freedom!
- *We must love the truth and believe the truth*, or be lost (II Thess. 2:10-12). Loving truth involves hating error and sin, as God does (6:16). There is a vast difference between right and wrong. We not only *can* but *must* discern the difference.
- *By the truth we will be judged* (Psa. 96:13).
- *Christ is the embodiment of truth:* "I am the way, the truth, and the life: no man cometh unto the Father, but by me" (Jno. 14:6).
- *Therefore, truth is not determined by majority concensus or by circumstances.* The rule must govern circumstances; circumstances do not create or govern the rule.

Truly, the Word is powerful! Living, active, sharper than a two-edged sword, effective, relevant, up-to-date, essential, exclusively absolute, dependable, and eternal. God's

Truth is Light for today! Showing us who we are, why we are, what to do, and where we are going. Nothing else can provide such a rewarding, lofty, intense purpose for living.

So we must hold to truth firmly and uncompromisingly — whatever the sacrifice. *"Buy the truth and sell it not."* To sell it is to sell one's own soul. A pitiful and tragic sale!

FOR THOUGHT OR DISCUSSION

- Words are powerful, but only as valid and believable as the credibility and authority of the speaker. Those who reject the Bible do so because they deny or doubt the authority of the Author. Even some who claim to believe the Bible are actually "practical atheists" — refusing to follow commandments with which they disagree. They want God on a stand-by basis, as a kind of fireman or policeman, to be called in case of emergency but inobstrusive at all other times.

- "Every word of God is pure ... Add thou not unto his words, lest he reprove thee, and thou be found a liar" (30:5,6). If we presume to alter His words in any way, we are actually presuming ourselves to be wiser than our Maker. See also Deut. 4:2; Gal. 1:8,9; II Jno. 9-11.

- To refuse divine instructions is to despise ourselves. "He that refuseth instruction despiseth his own soul" (15:32) — like a drowning man who refuses a lifeline and fancies he spites the thrower!

- Several years ago a school teacher attending required in-service training said the director wrote this statement on the blackboard: "Nothing is either good or evil. It is only as you think it is." No statement could be more false or anti-biblical. This thinking is wide-spread. Yet any person who accepts it is stripped of any basis whatever for morality, social justice, spiritual attainment, or any other excellence. Think about it!

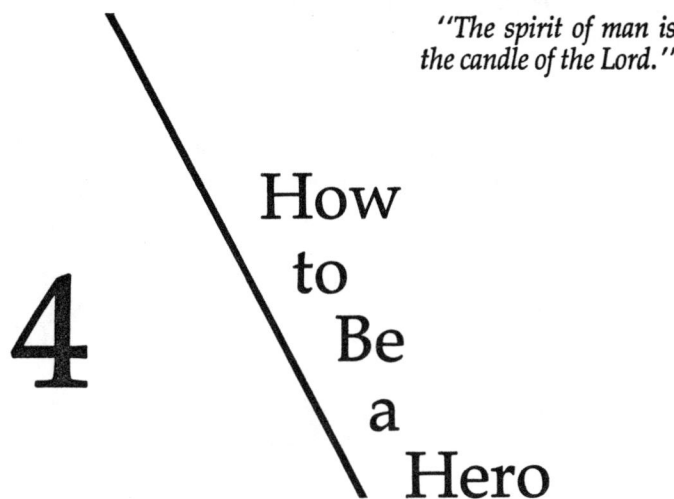

"The spirit of man is the candle of the Lord."

4 — How to Be a Hero

As a young father pushed a baby carriage through the park, he spoke above the infant's frantic cries: "Take it easy, Jimmy. Now everything's going to be all right. So, Jimmy, be calm." A woman passing by, thinking to comfort the young man with friendly conversation, said: "So your little boy is named Jimmy." "Oh, no," corrected the father. "His name is Fred. I'm Jimmy."

How priceless is self-mastery and self-control! So valuable that the Lord says the person who can rule his own spirit is better than "he that taketh a city" (16:32). Thus, the real hero is not the one who subdues physical cities, but the one who conquers the "city" within. Not an easy task — but a goal worth a lifetime of effort.

On the other hand, "He that hath no rule over his own spirit is like a city that is broken down and without walls" (25:28) — defenseless, deteriorating in shambles. An intriguing symbol: our inner being compared to a "city" with all sorts of "people" — constructive or destructive, law-abiding or lawless, quarrelsome or peaceful — oftentimes in conflict. Even the apostle Paul felt this inner struggle, so nobody is exempt (Rom. 7:15-25). Each person is a bundle of contradictory forces ranging from vicious to virtuous.

This conquest must begin with a self-audit to determine which "tenants" should be evicted, and which should be nurtured and strengthened. How can this be done? In another intriguing symbol, Wisdom says: "The spirit [intelligence, innate being] of man is the candle of the Lord, searching all the inward parts" (20:27). Can you visualize using a lighted candle to search every nook of your own heart, analyzing and appraising each trait and motive? This candle is our own spirit or mind — indeed a dim light, unless lighted by God's lamp which lets us see ourselves as we really are. This search is necessary for all who would be a real hero.

For what man knoweth the things of a man, save the spirit of man which is in him? (I Cor. 2:11).

Examine yourselves, whether ye be in the faith; prove your own selves (II Cor. 13:5).

"Keep Thy Heart With All Diligence"

Heart. Few words are more frequently used or more misunderstood. Perhaps this is because each person has two hearts, and it is easy to confuse the two.

Dr. Philip Blieberg, the world's first heart-transplant patient, was the first person ever to view his own physical heart. Yet, what he saw was merely a blood pump. When it was replaced, the real Dr. Blieberg was in no way altered. As God's word explains, man is two beings, with two hearts (II Cor. 4:16). One is the center of physical life, pumping blood to the body's extremities. The other is the life-center of the spiritual or inner man. This is the important one; but tragically, this kind of heart trouble is usually given little or no thought.

God defines the spiritual heart: that which thinks (Matt.

9:4), understands (Matt. 13:15), believes (Rom. 10:10), despises (II Sam. 6:16), loves (Matt. 22:37), and obeys (Rom. 6:17). A right relationship with God does not depend on the body's blood pump but on the health of the spiritual heart: proper understanding, belief, love, and obedience. So it is not located in the chest but in the head — the mind.

By this heart God sees and judges us. "The Lord seeth not as man seeth; for man looketh on the outward appearance, but the Lord looketh on the heart" (I Sam. 16:7). "The fining pot is for silver, and the furnace for gold; but the Lord trieth the hearts" (17:3).

So above all things: "Keep thy heart with all diligence." Why? It's the fountainhead of all conduct. "For out of it are the issues of life" (4:23). We are not what we think we are. Rather, what we THINK, we ARE. "As he thinketh in his heart, so is he" (23:7). Keeping the spiritual heart healthy is not easy or automatic. It requires a lifetime of deliberate, conscious effort. "Who can say, I have made my heart clean, I am pure from sin?" (20:9). It's a rhetorical question.

The heart is a solitary place, never completely shared with others. Understanding this helps to cope with loneliness and misunderstandings, even with those closest to us. "The heart knoweth his own bitterness; and a stranger doth not intermeddle with his joy" (14:10).

Not e'en the tenderest heart and next our own,
Knows half the reasons why we smile or sigh.
　　　　　　　　　　—Keble

Others can go only so far in sharing our joys and sorrows. The deepest feelings are buried in our heart's silent chambers. Each person is a solitary unit responsible for his eternal destiny, so cleansing our hearts is our duty and ours alone. But how consoling to know that our Omniscient Father sees, understands, and guides us in this task.

"Keep thy heart" is a commandment. God does not command the impossible, so it is possible to control the thoughts and will of the heart. Some who try to control their tongue exert little effort in thought-control. Yet, success or failure begins with thoughts. It's an inside job.

The Control Tower

Our space age has taught the necessity of a nerve center, a control tower, to direct air traffic. Think of the chaos and tragedies, if the controllers failed to perform their duties. Our heart, our thought center, is the control tower to direct our life's "traffic." A powerful blessing! Do we use it responsibly and constructively? Consider life's areas so controlled.

Thoughts and happiness are inseparably connected. Happiness dwells in the heart or not all, for it is an inward state, not an outward circumstance. A heart at ease with itself and its Maker is one of life's most cherished treasures.

Thoughts affect disposition. What thoughts absorbed your mind today? Each has been either a plus or a minus, constructive or destructive. "I wish I didn't have to . . ." "I'm disgusted . . ." "I don't like . . ." "I'm tired of . . ." "I can't . . ." Such thoughts turn us aside from life's lofty goals. Each day begins with a viewpoint, which not only affects disposition and sets the tone for the whole day, but has a direct bearing on all our associates.

> Two men looked out from prison bars.
> One saw mud; the other saw stars.
> —Author Unknown

The honey bee and the vulture fly over the same field. The bee finds flowers, and the vulture finds the corrupt carcass. Of course, they do so by instinct, but our Creator has given us the power to choose between the two. And our choice usually develops into a life-long habit. Will we adopt the "half-empty" or the "half-full" syndrome?

Thoughts affect health. Our bodies are sacred, the handiwork of God. Thoughts of discouragement, pessimism, anger, despair, envy, guilt, or frustration can be detrimental to health; so we must practice thought-control. A man who boasted of his explosive temper developed serious physical problems. His doctor told him not to get mad, that anger could kill him. What did he do? He controlled his temper! How? By controlling his thoughts, of course. His thought of survival was stronger than his desire to lash out at others.

Thoughts can overcome circumstances. Sooner or later everyone faces uncontrollable problems. Then we have only two alternatives: to adjust to the circumstances, or destroy ourselves by fighting against the inevitable.

Joseph, through no fault of his own, was sold into Egypt by envious brothers. How easily he could have spent his life consumed with hatred and bitterness. Instead, he leaned on the Lord and achieved an influential and productive life.

The apostle Paul endured physical torture, imprisonment, and betrayal by false brethren; but he said: "I have learned, in whatsoever state I am, therewith to be content" (Phil. 4:11). Contentment was *learned*. It began in his mind, his control tower.

Thoughts determine our moral and spiritual state. Remember: we BECOME what we put into our minds. It is not possible to constantly see, read, or hear that which is carnal and ungodly and then BECOME morally pure. Think of your family's conversations, books, magazines, television shows, movies, music, recreation. Do they increase or decrease spirituality?

Since every action, right or wrong, begins with a seed-thought, our Father tells us to cultivate thoughts that are honest, just, pure, lovely, of good report, virtuous, and praiseworthy

(Phil. 4:8). The mind is never a blank, but we choose what it absorbs. Nobody else! So my biggest problem is me. Your biggest problem is you. We only deceive ourselves if we believe otherwise.

The "Respectable" Sins

Sins of the heart are the "respectable" spiritual maladies, yet among the most insidious. Since they are hidden from others' view, it is easy to feel little challenge to evict these undesirable "tenants." After all, who will know — or even care — if we should win a battle within ourselves? With the Light of God's Word, let's use our own "candle" to search within.

Do we see selfishness — the mother of most sins? From the beginning, man has been tempted to partake of anything which promises pleasure, benefit, or exaltation. Love of self is a grievous sin (II Tim. 3:2). Rather, "Let every one of us please his neighbor for his good to edification. For even Christ pleased not himself" (Rom. 15:1-3). How thankful we should be! And He will give us strength to look beyond our selfish inclinations and build our lives on a loftier plane. He admonishes: "If any man will come after me, let him deny himself ..." (Matt. 16:24,25). Real living comes through self-denial, not self-indulgence. No person can practice both. The one we choose begins with an attitude and permeates the whole of living.

Do we see ingratitude? Just plain unthankfulness! But it is in God's list of vilest sins (II Tim. 3:2).

Ingratitude toward God pervades the earth, for many never look up to the Source of all blessings. Failing to return good for good is inexcusable, but returning evil for good is incredible vileness (17:13). However, failure to recognize and appreciate the goodness of God and fellowmen is more than thoughtless oversight and bad manners. It's evil! It's returning evil for good. Ingratitude is one sin of those whose "foolish heart is darkened" (Rom. 1:21). Surely we don't want to be in this group.

Yet, sadly, even God's people are so often guilty. Jeshurun had "waxed fat and grown thick" and then "forsook God which made him and lightly esteemed the Rock of his salvation ... Of the Rock that begat thee thou art unmindful, and hast forgotten God that formed thee" (Deut. 32:6-18). "Jeshurun" is a term signifying all God's people, so the weight of this is as relevant as ever.

It seems that prosperity (waxing fat and thick!) always breeds ingratitude. How unthinkable. Just the opposite should be true. We are indebted to God for life itself, for the air we breathe, the soil and sun and rain essential for food, even for the ability to love and enjoy all human relationships. Even more indispensable: He is the Rock of our salvation. So our first waking thought each day should be: "Thank you, Father."

Failure to feel or express gratitude stems from pride and ego. To say "Thank you" admits a debt to another, and many simply lack the humility to do so. Gratitude nurtures our own inner beauty and lifts the hearts of others. Why would anyone want to miss such a golden opportunity? How often do you thank God? Husband? Wife? Children? Friends? Parents? Try it! You'll like it! They will like it! And God will like it! Because He knows this is one aspect of spiritual growth.

Do we find pride? It's one of the Lord's most-hated sins (6:17; 8:13; 21:4). Humility does not mean self-depreciation or weakness. Rather, it is understanding our dependence on God and fellowmen, while pride is an exaggerated opinion of self-sufficiency and self-worth. Pride brings self-destruction (29:23; 16:18). In all areas, injured pride is a major cause of contention (13:10). Then the injured one tends to retaliate, perhaps not even realizing the real reason.

Pride also brings shame (11:2). Think of the hurt! To be brought low for all the world to see. Read one example

(25:6,7). So Wisdom says: "Be smart; avoid this humiliation by practicing humility."

Do we see covetousness? It's a sin that God calls idolatry (Col. 3:5). So what is it? The dictionary defines covetous: "very desirous, especially of another's property; grasping; avaricious; having unlawful desire."

Wisdom warns that covetousness can lead to murder (1:19). Any covetous family member can envelop the entire household in turmoil (15:27). The world is filled with people who don't want to put forth the necessary effort to acquire things they desire; so they blame others, feel mistreated, and greedily covet what others have (21:25,26).

The love of money causes some to err from the faith and drown themselves in destruction and perdition (I Tim. 6:9,10). Wealth has no character of its own, good or evil, but takes on the character of its owner. It is the *love* of money, not money, which is the root of evil. God "giveth us richly all things to enjoy," but they must be kept in proper perspective. Material things can be either a blight or a blessing, depending on our attitude and use of them. Even the very poor can be guilty of idolatry through covetousness.

Do we see envy — one of the strongest, yet most prevalent, of all emotions? It is an all-pervading destructive force, the cancer of the spiritual heart. "A sound heart is the life of the flesh: but envy is the rottenness of the bones" (14:30). Then what is envy? A feeling of uneasiness or unhappiness over others' accomplishments — whether possessions, position, or popularity. Christ's crucifixion was caused by envy (Matt. 27:18). Cain's envy prompted him to kill his brother Abel (Gen. 4:3-16). These examples help define the sin. Religious leaders were violently disturbed over Christ's popularity with the people. Cain's unhappiness over the fact that God accepted Abel's sacrifice reached murderous intensity. Neither murder was caused by possessions, though envy can surely involve materialism.

"Wrath is cruel, and anger is outrageous: but who is able to stand before envy?" (27:4). Time may cool anger, but envy smoulders continually, ever ready to burst into flames. Envy is a sure sign of a lack of love, for love and envy cannot dwell in the same heart (I Cor. 13:4).

Do we hate scripturally? To love completely requires learning to hate properly. Love is powerful. So is hatred. Both are exemplified by our Creator, and we are admonished to be "followers of God, as dear children" (Eph. 5:1). What is the "perfect hatred" spoken of by the Psalmist (Psa. 139:22)? It is to love what God loves, and to hate what God hates. Man's tendency, however, is to reverse this order. There is hatred forbidden, and hatred commanded. Learning and practicing the difference is essential.

What kind of hatred is condemned? "He that despiseth his neighbor sinneth" (14:21). Envy is the daughter of pride and the mother of hatred. Esau envied Jacob, hated, and then vowed to kill him. Hatred disrupts all society. Those who despise others live in a despicable world, for hatred is a boomerang which returns to harm the despiser more than the despised. Indeed, the cost of hating is too high. It isn't worth it. Yet it is a common tendency. Even those not totally filled with hatred must guard against contempt or distaste for others. Oftentimes:

The poor despise the rich, and the rich the poor.

The unlearned despise the educated, and the educated the unlearned.

The immoral despise the moral, and the moral the immoral.

What kind of hatred is commanded? The Psalmist said: "I hate every false way" (Psa. 119:104). — not the sinner, but the sinner's false way. In this, the Psalmist was following the Father whose hatred of evil and false ways is clearly specified in *Proverbs*, as cited in our studies. Is this inconsistent with the fact that God is love? Not at all. In fact, it is a necessary component of love. It is not possible to endorse righteousness without condemning unrighteousness, or to uphold sobriety without opposing drunkenness. It is not possible to love God's way without hating ways that oppose and contradict Him.

So we should hate — not people, but evil and every false way. In fact, love for souls demands that we hate evil and strive to lead people out of its path. Mankind's weakness is a tendency to hate people and condone *false ways* — doctrines which contradict God's way or teaching. So we should seriously ask ourselves: Are we spiritually mature? Do we hate scripturally?

Hate the evil, and love the good (Amos 5:15).

Abhor that which is evil; cleave to that which is good (Rom. 12:9).

Our hearts should be examined for other traits, some of which are discussed in chapters to follow.

Example of a Hero

David is a shining example of heroic living, being called a man after God's own heart. How could this be said of one who committed grievous sins? The answer is found in his attitude toward God, himself, and his sin. When he realized his sin, he was immediately ready and anxious to repent and make amends, to be restored to fellowship with the Father.

The essence of David's heart is movingly revealed: "Search me, O God, and know my heart, try me, and know my thoughts, and see if there be any wicked way in me, and lead me in the way everlasting" (Psa. 139:23,24). Of course, God already knew David's heart, but this shows his attitude. He wanted above all things for his *thoughts* and *ways* to be acceptable to the Father, to whom he looked for leadership "in the way everlasting."

Likewise, we should muster the courage to make such a search of our inner "city" — to nurture the lofty and desirable "tenants" while ousting the undesirables. This is real heroism — more notable than conquering cities. Cities perish with time; our spirits live forever.

FOR THOUGHT OR DISCUSSION

- Booker T. Washington, honored black American scientist, said: "I shall allow no man to belittle my soul by making me hate him." If we hate or envy, we are allowing another to control our lives, damaging ourselves most of all.

- No person is born with gratitude. Just as children must be reminded repeatedly to comb their hair, close the door, etc., they should be coached and trained to say "Thank you." If not, they become ungrateful adults. A woman who sent gifts to eleven high school graduates, all Christians, said she received thanks from THREE of them! This reveals gross sin and neglect by the parents as well as the students.

- Words of pride are foolish and self-defeating. "In the mouth of the foolish is a rod of pride" (14:3). The braggart defeats his own purpose — lowering, not exalting, self in the minds of others. Conceit or self-righteousness should not exist in the heart, but to express such is indeed foolish and inexcusable.

- Pride prompts some people to frequently point out their own inadequacies for the purpose of causing others to contradict them and counter with a compliment, though the speaker may not even be conscious of the underlying motive.

- The apostle Paul said: "I can do all things." A proud boast? No, for in the next phrase he specified the basis of his strength: "through Christ which strengtheneth me" (Phil. 4:13). Confidence is not synonymous with pride. The difference is in understanding and crediting the Source of all ability and accomplishments.

- Some people are like the man who said: "I used to be conceited, but now I don't have any faults at all."

- Sometimes envy is confused with covetousness. Many, many times people envy (feel unhappy and disgruntled over another's position, popularity, or possessions) without coveting that thing. For instance, if you had a luxurious yacht (or even a sail boat!) I surely would not want it (covet it). Large bodies of water do not entice me; but if I should feel unhappy and distressed *because you have it, that is envy.*

- One profitable spiritual exercise is to study passages in *Proverbs* which specify things abominable to God (3:32; 6:16,19; 11:1; 12:22; 15:8,9; 15:26; 16:5; 28:9).

Quotes to Consider

> Blessed are they who die for God,
> And earn the martyr's crown of light;
> Yet he who lives for God may be
> A greater conquerer in his sight.

It costs more to avenge injuries than to bear them.

He that keeps malice harbors a viper in his breast.

Meddle not with dirt; some of it will stick to you. — Danish proverb

He who swells in prosperity will shrink in adversity.

> Two principles in human nature reigns.
> Self-love to urge and reason to restrain.

Like a postage stamp, a man's value depends on his ability to stick to a thing till he gets there. — Joseph Chamberlain

He mourns the dead who lives as they desire. — Young
Pity cureth envy.

Rashness brings success to few, misfortune to many.

What cannot be cured must be endured. — Latin proverb

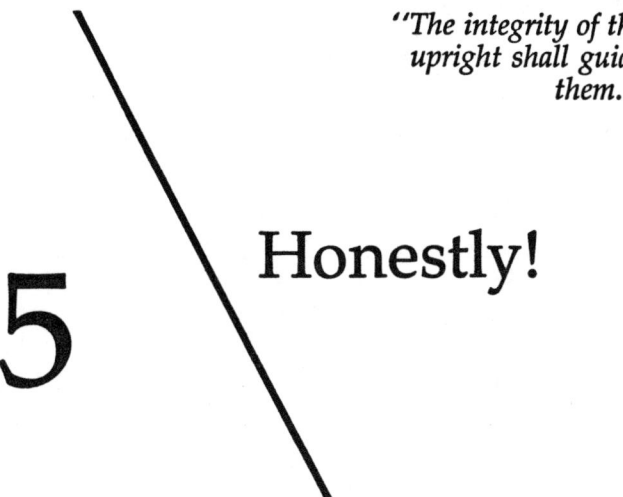

"The integrity of the upright shall guide them."

5 Honestly!

A small boy, selling berries from house to house, found a buyer. "Take the basket into your house and measure out a quart," he said. "But aren't you afraid I will take too many?" the lady asked. "No," he said, "I don't worry about that. Even if you did, I'd only lose a few berries; but you would make yourself a dishonest person, and I don't think you want to do that." What wisdom!

Better is the poor that walketh in his integrity, than he that is perverse in his lips, and is a fool (19:1).
Deceit is in the heart of them that imagine evil (12:20).
A false balance is abomination to the Lord: but a just weight is his delight (11:1).

What is honesty? The dictionary says: "absence of deceit; uprightness; integrity." What is dishonesty? Any deliberate attempt to deceive, to make things appear different from what they are. This may be done by action or word, overtly or by implication and innuendo.

Why Be Honest?

What's in it for me? A common reaction, not altogether to be condemned, for God motivates us by outlining rewards and penalties. A popular viewpoint is that total honesty is naive and stupid, that dishonesty can be a harmless means of achieving worthwhile goals. The question is: what does God think about it? A look beneath the surface shows why He has commanded integrity. It is the foundation of all other virtues. Without it, there is no basis for the character essential to successful living.

Dishonesty destroys self-respect. A person may hide devious motives and dishonest deeds from others; but if he sees a dishonest person in the mirror each day, he can feel nothing but contempt — unless his moral sensibilities have been totally destroyed.

Dishonesty destroys peace of mind. "Bread of deceit is sweet to a man; but afterwards his mouth shall be filled with gravel" (20:17). The good time, the triumph of fattening one's purse by outwitting another, the "sweet vengeance" of destroying another's good standing — whatever accomplished by the deception — later turns to gravel in one's mouth. An unexpected turn of events! Alone with one's conscience, gravel doesn't taste so good. So that isn't a smart thing to do, is it? One may escape the law, or even society's censure, but there's no place to hide from self — or from God.

Dishonesty destroys trust, damaging precious relationships which must be built on mutual trust: friendships, business relationships, marriage, and other family ties. Think about it. If someone lies to you, or deceives you, how does it affect you? Trust is something like "Humpty Dumpty." Once crushed by that "fall from the wall," putting it together again is almost impossible. Integrity, the relationship's foundation, has been damaged or perhaps destroyed. Is it worth the risk? This is one important reason for marital fidelity. Infidelity can leave a shattered empty shell. No wonder God beseeches: "Be faithful." It's necessary for the trust that undergirds happy relationships.

If a business partner lies or steals from you, how long can your relationship survive? Look at the enormous price paid for dishonesty! Is it worth it? The Golden Rule is the best rule: "Whatsoever ye would that men should do to you do ye even so to them" (Matt. 7:12).

Dishonesty destroys the soul, for it is an abomination to God (11:1; 20:10; 13:11). Therefore, the most serious consequences are eternal.

Then why do so many people practice dishonesty? One answer is forcefully given: "Because sentence against an evil work is not executed speedily, therefore the heart of the sons of men is fully set in them to do evil" (Eccl. 8:11). People think they are getting away with sin, simply because God does not strike them dead or punish them immediately. But note the Scripture. Sentencing is delayed, but not cancelled! To ignore this fact compounds self-deception.

Honesty is not just a policy. It is a principle which must permeate every facet of life. Honesty does not come in degrees. Dishonesty in little matters is no little matter. He that will steal a penny would steal a million, if circumstances permitted and punishment could be avoided.

Seeing its importance, the truly wise and successful person will practice honesty in all things.

Honesty in Thinking and Dealing With Others

This is fairness. Abraham Lincoln, known for his honesty and fairness, refused to legally represent clients he believed to be wrong. As President, he always considered his opponents' views. His enemies did not like him, but they respected and trusted him — a far greater tribute.

Being fair with others is simply the Golden Rule in action — treating others as we would be treated, free from devious motives or conduct. This honesty in judgment of others is far more serious than many have suspected. To justify and condone others' sinful conduct is wrong, an abomination to God. So is the condemnation of a just person. Though this is often done, Wisdom teaches:

He that justifieth the wicked, and he that condemneth the just, even they both are abomination to the Lord. (17:15).

Another unfair aspect of dealing with others, closely related to the above, is prejudice and hasty conclusions. Prejudice means to pre-judge, to reach a conclusion before examining the evidence. "He that answereth a matter before he heareth it, it is folly and shame to him" (18:13). Yet, it's easy to do: to judge others on the slightest acquaintance or to judge a friend's conduct without sufficient knowledge about the matter, to discipline children without hearing all the facts, to form religious views before examining what God has to say on the subject. Whatever the realm, Wisdom calls this foolish and shameful.

Suppose a civil judge should come to the courtroom some morning and say to the bailiff: "I'm going golfing this morning, but I have written my decision concerning today's case. You will find it in my desk drawer." How would we react? No doubt we would quickly respond: "That's ridiculous, dishonest, and unthinkable. The judge hasn't even heard the evidence pro or con. How can he possibly render a proper decision?" So we must be very careful lest we fall into this error.

Honest in Speech

The wicked heart uses words to deceive, to make things appear what they are not.

Burning lips and a wicked heart are like a potsherd covered with silver dross . . . when he speaketh fair, believe him not (26:23-26).

A potsherd is a broken piece of pottery. Who would think of having it silver-plated? Only a person desiring to deceive, to make it appear something it is not. How are words so used?

Hypocritical words are designed for ulterior aims — "silver dross" which covers nothing more valuable than a worthless potsherd (11:9). "Deceive not with thy lips" (24:28).

Lying is calculated to deceive — to cover conduct one wishes to hide, to exalt self, to shift blame from self to others, to effect some material gain, or other self-serving aims.

How serious is this sin? Satan is the father of all lies (Jno. 8:44).

Lying lips are an abomination to the Lord: but they that deal truly are his delight (12:22).

A faithful witness will not lie: but a false witness will utter lies (14:5).

All liars shall have their part in the lake of fire which burneth with fire and brimstone: which is the second death (Rev. 21:8).

It would be hard to misunderstand these verses. Lying can destroy the soul! Yet, for many today, lying has become almost as natural as breathing. In any situation, they do not measure their words by the standard: "What is true?" but rather: "What would others like to hear?" or "What will accomplish my purpose?" Deceit becomes a daily way of life. With their conscience hardened, they never stop to realize they have destroyed the very foundation of their character: integrity.

Flattery is another deceptive devise of evil people (2:16). This is one strategy used by designing women (7:21) and devious men with a "line." What is flattery? Any compliment? No, for a compliment may reflect sincere kindness and a desire to encourage. Then what is flattery? The key is the motive. Though the words may be true, one who compliments for the purpose of exalting self, or gaining some favor, is guilty of flattery. A flatterer may "speak fair" while "there are seven abominations in his heart" (26:25).

Therefore, meddle not with him that flattereth with his lips (20:19).

Bearing false witness is lying about someone rather than *to* someone.

A man that beareth false witness against his neighbor is a maul, and a sword, and a sharp arrow (25:18).

Three instruments of destruction: maul, sword, and arrow. So how can a person destroy his neighbor — his good name, his reputation, his peace of mind? By telling that which is not true.

Honesty in Business

To steal, to defraud, to take unfair advantage, violates another's right to use and enjoy that for which he has worked. So we are not surprised to read:

A false balance is abomination to the Lord (11:1).

Subtle or secret fraud is as evil as open robbery, and even more cowardly. The escalation of "white collar crime" is appalling. Some disdain to label themselves a thief, if the thievery can be practiced covertly while remaining in the good graces of associates and society. They would be horrified at the thought of holding up a bank, looting a jewelry store, or taking money by force — yet feel no hesitancy at altering the scales or computer records, changing the gasoline pumps, selling one product and installing an inferior one, cheating on a business transaction, stealing from an employer, or misrepresenting merchandise on a sale. All are acts of thievery, and, according to our text, abominable in God's sight.

Such dishonesty is often shrugged off with a flippant excuse: "Oh, everybody shades deals to his own advantage." Run from the person who so speaks, for it is the key to his entire character. Though dishonesty is common, the person who believes that "everybody does it" indicts himself. A liar thinks all are liars. A thief believes that all others steal. An honest person, however, *knows* that *"everybody" doesn't* practice dishonesty.

Buyers (customers) also have an obligation to be honest (20:14), a problem more prevalent in the days of direct bargaining, but an admonition still needed. Buyers have an obligation to sellers who must make a profit or else close their business. What if there were no merchants from whom to buy? So justice demands a fair profit for the seller. One who tends a vineyard is entitled to the profit (I Cor. 9:7) if we want him to continue to supply fruit. "The laborer is worthy of his hire" (Lk. 10:7). This includes merchants (employers). Trying to squeeze them down to a pauper's pittance would not only violate Christian principles but would in the long run harm the consumer most of all.

Employee honesty is a constant responsibility, but theft by employees has become a national scandal involving millions of dollars. This loss must be borne by the customers, increasing everyone's cost of living. How can anyone justify this sin? In principle, it is the same as robbing at gunpoint. As already mentioned, since it is done deceptively and undercover, isn't it even more cowardly? Employees also steal from employers in another way: by wasting or misusing time. Stealing time from an employer is just as dishonest as stealing goods.

A failure to pay debts is dishonest. Yet some people congratulate themselves on their ability to outsmart the bill collectors. "Owe no man anything" (Rom. 13:8). To the person of integrity, meeting financial obligations is as natural as breathing. He would never consider doing otherwise. *Dishonesty in all forms has always been condemned.* Centuries ago God's law stated that one who lied about things entrusted to him, or about finding lost property, was guilty of sin. The deceiver was required to restore full-fold plus twenty percent (Lev. 6:2-5).

Honesty in Religion

Surely nobody denies that much deception is disguised as religion, one of Satan's most powerful methods. Since people are conditioned to think that any religion is good, Satan can easily "transform himself into an angel of light" and deceive millions. And he is surely taking advantage of his opportunity. In our "intellectual age" the devil has gone out of fashion — but he hasn't gone out of business! He has his churches, his ministers, and his disciples (II Cor. 11:13-15). Overt Satan worship is not the total of Satan's work by any means.

How can we recognize the devil's work? By measuring every teaching by Divine Truth, the Word of God (Jno. 17:17). Doctrines devised by human beings produce vain worship (Matt. 15:9). And truth misinterpreted and misapplied is a "wresting of the Scriptures" resulting in spiritual destruction (II Pet. 3:15-17).

One of Satan's most popular "lines" is that there is no difference between truth and error, right and wrong, honesty and dishonesty — no absolutes, leaving each person free to set his own standards and "do his own thing." This doctrine is contrary not only to God's word but even to common sense. We must diligently examine all teachings. The stakes are too high to risk being led astray by false teachers. So we must be honest in our relationship with God, in doctrine and practice.

What Honesty Can't Do

Some have ascribed to honesty a power it does not possess. How? In recent years it has become popular to reason that *anything goes*, just as long as a person openly admits it. "Tell it like it is" has become for some their total and only moral commitment. No doubt the prevalence of hypocrisy contributed to the growth of this attitude; but to fall into the ditch on the other side of the immoral road solves nothing.

In some circles it is the "in" thing to say: "Of course, we have a 'live-in relationship' but at least we're honest about it; we're not hypocrites." The implication is that any conduct, no matter how unacceptable to God or society, is suddenly and automatically made right as long as it is admitted. This would ascribe to *honesty* the power to whitewash sin, to turn wrong into right. *Honesty has no such power!*

Think for a moment. How does anyone know that honesty is right, that dishonesty, or being a hypocrite, is wrong? Only by God's revelation. The same Guide, however, which forbids hypocrisy also forbids adultery, fornication, drunkenness, homosexuality, and many other deeds which some seek to whitewash with a layer of "honesty" — simply admitting the sin, or even boasting of it.

What is the necessary conclusion? The mere admission of sin does not neutralize it or make it right. Wrong can be covered only by the blood of Christ, by following his conditions of forgiveness. Honesty alone cannot save any person from the inevitable consequences of sinful conduct.

For instance, the person who abuses his or her body with alcohol or other drugs may dismiss it lightly: "At least I'm honest about it; I admit it." But this honesty is powerless to prevent the inevitable consequences: destruction of the user's body and mind, and a soul unfit for eternity (Gal. 5:21).

So let's be careful not to depend on honesty to whitewash sinful and destructive conduct. *Let's "tell it like it is!" Honesty is essential — but honesty alone is not enough!* So why be honest? To summarize: honesty or integrity is a commandment of God, a violation of which has eternal consequences. However, even those who reject God should see the value of honesty in all things, for it is essential in building respect. Surely, goals worth all the effort!

FOR THOUGHT OR DISCUSSION

- Does installment buying violate the admonition to "owe no man anything?" No. Installment buying is a contract between buyer and seller, due at stated times. When the obligation is due, the honest person pays or makes satisfactory arrangements with his creditor.

- Have we ever been guilty of "condemning the just?" Have we ever heard an evil report about someone, judged and condemned that person in our own mind, later to learn the report to be totally false? How cautious we should be. No doubt this is the reason for the admonition to charge someone of evil only "at the mouth of two or three witnesses" (I Tim. 5:19). This is fairness in action, which accrues to our benefit and protects others.

- Customers or employees who steal from a large store often attempt to justify themselves by saying: "Oh, well, it's a big store with lots of money; they'll never miss it." That is totally beside the point! That in no way softens the sin or turns wrong into right. It is thievery just as surely as if taken at gun-point. It taints the thief's soul, though the merchant may never find out about it.

- One example of self-deception is given in Galatians 6:3: "For if a man thinketh himself to be something, when he is nothing, he deceiveth himself." Who determines who is *nothing* and who is *something*? Christ aids our analysis of true greatness:

Whosoever will be great among you, let him be your minister; and whosoever will be chief among you, let him be your servant: even as the Son of man came not to be ministered unto, but to minister, and to give his life a ransom for many (Matt. 26:28).

Do we ever honestly ask ourselves: is this *my standard of greatness? my goal in life?* Or have I been deceived into accepting the world's measurement of who is *something* and who is *nothing?*

- All hypocrisy is dishonesty. For an enlightening spiritual-growth study, make a list of every Scripture concerning hypocrisy (use your concordance).

- Self-deception is perhaps one of the most prevalent forms of deception — yet the most difficult to recognize and correct. Why? One who is deceived doesn't realize it. If so, it wouldn't be deception, but a matter of knowledge and deliberate action. Then how can we detect self-deception? Only by measuring ourselves by the Creator's fixed and certain standard. So BEING HONEST WITH SELF is one of our gravest responsibilities.

- Another example of self-deception: "Be ye doers of the word, and not hearers only, deceiving your own selves" (Jas. 1:22). It is easy to convince ourselves that if we *know* the will of God and Christ, then all is well with our souls. Dangerous self-deception!

    To him that knoweth to do good, and doeth it not, to him it is sin. (Jas. 4:17).

    Some who once knew and followed the Lord's way have abandoned it and returned to the world. Read Inspiration's heart-rending description of their tragic spiritual condition (II Pet. 3:20-22).

- What is self-righteousness? The person who adopts the attitude: *"I know* the Bible forbids so-and-so, but *I think it's all right."* In essence this is declaring SELF to be righteous, while admitting rejection and disregard for God's law. Such is self-deception. "Little children, let no man deceive you: he that doeth righteousness is righteous" (I Jno. 3:7). How do we "do righteousness?" "All thy commandments are righteousness" (Psa. 119:172).

Quotes to Consider

Truth is the foundation of all knowledge, and the cement of all societies. — Dryden

The good man alone is free and all bad men are slaves. — Maxim of the Stoics

Truth is seen as well as heard.

As a wolf is like a dog, so is a flatterer like a friend.

Wicked men cannot be friends, either among themselves or with the good. — Socrates

There is not much to a man who is not wiser today than yesterday. — Lincoln

She that loseth her modesty and honesty hath nothing else worth losing.

Those who believe money can do everything are frequently prepared to do everything for money.

> A single penny fairly got,
> Is worth a thousand that are not.
> —German proverb

Business may be troublesome, but idleness is pernicious.

The smallest bark on life's tumultuous ocean
  Will leave a track behind forevermore;
The lightest wave of influence, once in motion,
  Extends and widens to the eternal shore.
We should be wary, then who go before,
A myriad yet to be, and we should take
  Our bearings carefully where breakers roar
And fearful tempests gather: one mistake
May wreck unnumbered barks that follow in our wake.
—Sarah Knowles Bolton

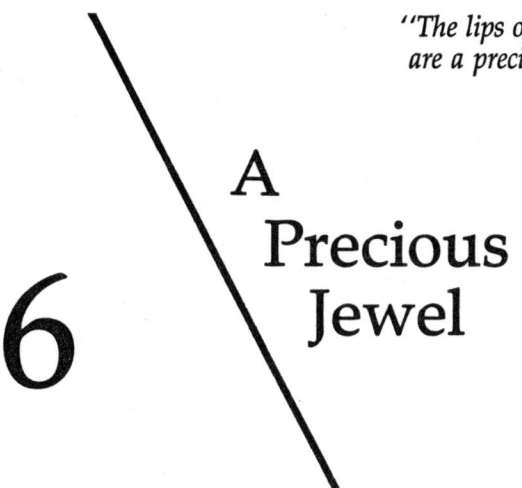

"The lips of knowledge are a precious jewel."

6 — A Precious Jewel

Words can be immortal. Many are. Words are vehicles by which thoughts and feelings are carried from one spirit to another. Whether good or bad, oftentimes they sink into the hearer's heart and live forever. Think of your departed loved ones. What comes first to your mind? Most likely their words, words so deeply engraved that they will forever remain a part of you. Long after we have forgotten our words, they continue to build up or tear down others. And for us, our words have eternal consequences. A loving Savior forewarns: "For by thy words thou shalt be justified, and by thy words thou shalt be condemned" (Matt. 12:37).

Self-mastery requires conquest over body and spirit, and the most unruly member is the tongue. To conquer it is such a glorious victory that God labels the victor a "perfect man" (Jas. 3:2) — that is, spiritually mature. This is the challenge and the possibility. Since speech is the barometer of the heart's condition, it broadcasts to the whole world whether we are winning or losing the battle within.

Thus, it is not possible to over-emphasize the importance

and power, the benefit or harm, of what we say. And nowhere is this more pungently, yet eloquently, described than in *Proverbs*. One profitable and revealing enterprise is to read the book, marking every verse involving speech. Note just a few.

The Tongue's Power to Destroy

Power to destroy what? Peace, love, reputations, marriages, friendships, and self-respect. The most treasured relationships of life can be killed with words. More tragic, however, is the tongue's power to destroy souls.

A fool's mouth is his destruction, and his lips are the snare of his soul (18:7).
Death and life are in the power of the tongue (18:21).
He that openeth wide his lips shall have destruction (13:3).
A hypocrite with his mouth destroyeth his neighbour (11:9).
The wicked is snared by the transgression of his lips (12:13).
Lying lips are abomination to the Lord (12:22).

An ancient secular proverb observes: "Men, because of speech, have the advantage over brutes; but beasts are preferable to men whose language is indecent."

The tongue is likened to a fire — denoting power to cause pain, anguish, destruction, and death. "An ungodly man diggeth up evil: and in his lips there is as a burning fire" (16:27). See also James 3:6-8. The damage wrought by fire is never fully known until the flames have ceased and a total estimate is made. Likewise, it is not possible to know the full extent of tongue-destruction until the final accounting on the day of judgment.

Words can be as sharp as a sword (12:18), as keen as a razor (Psa. 52:2). Have you ever been so heart-wounded that the scars will remain forever? What weapon wielded the devastating blow? Probably it was words. Nothing can wound deeper. Some seek to veil their sarcastic darts with wit, congratulating themselves on their cleverness. They only deceive themselves. The hearers easily see through the ruse, and the "clever joker" loses much in respect and esteem. Wit at the expense of others is the lowest form of conversation.

Tempting words, designed to lead others into sin, have always been a powerful tool of evil men and women, causing spiritual destruction for both the enticer and the enticed. "My son, if sinners entice thee, consent thou not. If they say, Come with us . . ." (1:10-16). See also 16:29,30 and 5:3. Sinners love companionship, aid, and comfort. So all who seek the good life must be constantly on guard against such verbal persuasion.

Strife begins with words, almost always. " As coals are to burning coals, and wood to fire: so is a contentious man to kindle strife" (26:21). "A froward man soweth strife" (16:28). Trouble always travels with the one who loves to quarrel. Such a person "calleth for strokes" (18:6) — enjoys a verbal battle much more than peace, viewing most situations as a challenge to pit argumentative skills against others and strive to emerge as victor.

One who is "soon angry" lives in an angry world, for others tend to respond in kind. Anger prompts any person to "deal foolishly" with words that generate more heat than light (14:17; 12:16). Psychologists conclude there are only three basic causes of anger, whether in adults or children:

- Wounded pride — others thinking less of us than we think we deserve.
- Blocked behavior — being prevented from doing something we want to do.
- Injustices to ourselves or others, both real and imagined.

There is a time for anger. Christ exemplified this — not when he was maligned personally, but when principles of the Father were attacked (Matt. 21:12). So surely Christ's followers should view error with indignation which prompts action. Without a potential for temper, gentleness is mere cowardice. One who never becomes angry has never contemplated the world's injustices and needs. However, the wise will "defer anger" (19:11) — take time to weigh their words' consequences, rather than speaking that which they would never approve in calmer moments. "He that is slow to anger is better than the mighty" (16:32). So anger is at times justified, but how careful we should be lest it lead us into sin. "Be angry and sin not" (Eph. 4:26). Anger is a wonderful servant but a terrible master.

"In the multitude of words there wanteth not sin: but he that refraineth his lips is wise" (10:19). Since we must talk daily, it is easy to talk too much and thereby become ensnared in sin.

He that hath knowledge spareth words . . . even a fool, when he holdeth his peace, is counted wise: and he that shutteth his lips is esteemed a man of understanding (17:27,28).

A fool uttereth all his mind (29:11).

People who boast, "I say everything I think" are no doubt unaware that they brand themselves as fools according to God's standard. To exercise restraint, especially under provocation, is one sign of wisdom and maturity. There is a "time to be silent" (Eccl. 3:7). When?

- When we are angry, using time to regain composure and choose words.
- When another is angry, allowing time for wrath to cool.
- When we are ignorant on the subject under consideration. So many people talk when they simply

do not know what they are talking about. Since even the righteous Job was guilty of speaking "words without knowledge" (Job 38:2) how careful we should be!

Talebearing seems to be a favorite hobby of some. It's a "respectable" sin, engaged in freely by people who never realize its seriousness. Yet, the talebearer is a walking incendiary, spreading the fires of strife and heartache.

Where no wood is, there the fire goeth out; so where there is no talebearer, the strife ceaseth (26:20).

A talebearer revealeth secrets; but he that is of a faithful spirit concealeth the matter (11:13).

A whisperer separateth chief friends (16:28).

The words of a talebearer are as wounds (26:22).

The same word is translated "talebearer" or "whisperer," shedding light on the meaning. Any secret entrusted to us, or "whispered" words which could harm, should never be passed on to others. Though thoughtlessly and carelessly repeated, the damage is done.

Fault-finding requires no talent whatsoever. Anyone can do it! It's easy to identify others' "warts," to magnify them, and use them to pit friend against friend. Though malice may not be the intent, the result is the same: causing strife or even destroying reputations. One who follows the law of love does not rejoice in evil. Though he sees others' faults, he does not enjoy sharing such "juicy tidbits."

Wisdom also warns that meddling words will bring trouble to the meddler. "He that passeth by, and meddleth with strife belonging not to him, is like one that taketh a dog by the ears" (26:17). It isn't always easy to discern the fine line of distinction between meddling and thoughtful aid, but we should surely try.

"How Good Is It!"

"A word in due season, how good is it!" (15:23). Speaking the right word at the right time. What a lovely art! One which can be learned by anyone. There is a "due season." Words perfectly fitting at one time may be altogether out of order at another time. A common sense principle. A raincoat is quite useful at times, but to wear it in the burning sun would be not only ludicrous but painful. So is it with words. *"The lips of the righteous know what is acceptable"* (10:32).

"The lips of the righteous feed many" (10:21), *and how the world needs this nourishment!* Just as fire and water have enormous potential for good or harm, so do words. They can be destructive. On the other hand, nothing is more comforting, uplifting, sweet, or precious than right words.

The tongue of the just is as choice silver (10:20).

Pleasant words are as a honeycomb, sweet to the soul, and health to the bones (16:24).

There is gold, and a multitude of rubies: but the lips of knowledge are a precious jewel (20:15).

A word fitly spoken is like apples of gold in pictures of silver (25:11).

Words of cheer and encouragement are so needed and valuable. Many hearts reel from severe blows, dashed hopes, or tormenting depression. "Heaviness in the heart of man maketh it stoop; but a good word maketh it glad" (12:25). A good word! Discouragement is such a common ailment. Most people are waging an uphill battle. Some are on the verge of losing. Whatever the cause, how keenly they need someone to shed light on what seems to be an unbearably dark pathway ahead. A good word in due season can work wonders to heal the hurting heart, lighten the heavy load, dispel gloomy despair, instill hope and confidence. This is the power of Christ, and the privilege of Christians — to help others understand that the joy of the Lord makes the bright days brighter and the dark days bearable.

Words of praise and appreciation. How good they are! Deep within each heart is a need for approval and applause. Children blossom under the sunlight of praise. Since censure is a necessary part of discipline, it must be tempered with commendation or a child becomes increasingly discouraged and unsure of himself. In Bible class one day a mother explained that she had resolved never to go through a day without commending each child for something. She cited a recent day when her little boy had tried her patience almost to the breaking point. She said: "As I was putting him to bed that night, I really had to work hard to think of something worthy of praise, but I did it!"

For the elderly, appreciation is wonderfully welcome and therapeutic. Those who have outlived many loved ones and friends often feel intense loneliness and uselessness, and are surely in need of a good word.

Words of hope and comfort to the faint-hearted is a constant need. For instance, a person scheduled for serious surgery is apprehensive, needing strength and courage to face the inevitable. Keenly in need of a good word. Suppose some visitor, some would-be "comforter" should say: "You know, my aunt had the very same symptoms. She survived the surgery but died a few months later." Surely a word out of season!

Or suppose someone "comforts" a grieving widow: "I hate to tell you this, but you will miss him more as time goes on. I know. I've been through the same thing, and you can't imagine all the problems ahead of you." A word out of season. As Job observed, such people are indeed "miserable comforters." Silence is often the best comforter, speaking far more eloquently than any words. Without a doubt, a simple concerned presence — with silence — is preferable to a word *out of season.*

Words of sympathy. "Sympathy" means "to feel with." Whether the burden is grief, illness, disappointment, economic hardship, or any other agony, we need someone to say: "I understand, and I want to help lighten your load." So the Golden Rule demands that we sense this need in others, ever sensitive to speak a good word in due season.

Words to promote peace. Enemies, friends, or relatives may speak at times in anger, bitterness, or irritation. To reply in kind would only multiply the problem, causing a little spark to become a great flame, but "a soft answer turneth away wrath" (15:1).

Words of gratitude are a necessary part of the good life, discussed more fully in Chapter 4. Just a simple "Thank you" has the power to lift another's spirits and beautify our own. Yet, how many times have we neglected opportunities to do so?

The powerful impact of words should prompt us to hesitate before we speak, trying to discern the reaction on others. This requires foresight, self-discipline, and insight into human nature. Our tendency is to speak from our own feelings at the time. Angry words may quickly rise from our own taut nerves. Melancholy words may spring from our own despondency. Bitter words may stem from our own disappointments. Our mood is probably transitory, but the words born therefrom will be permanent in the minds of hearers and more far-reaching than we can imagine. So no wonder Wisdom observes: "The heart of the righteous studieth to answer" (15:28).

Little packages of power. It has been suggested that in dealing with others, there are simple words with immense power. If learned early, these can promote life-long blessings. Consider the possibilities and the impact.

The ONE most powerful word: "Please."

The TWO most powerful words: "Thank you."
The THREE most powerful words: "I love you."
The FOUR most powerful words: "What do you think?"
The FIVE most powerful words: "I am proud of you."

Words To Use Knowledge Aright

"The tongue of the wise useth knowledge aright" (15:2). "The lips of the wise disperse knowledge" (15:7), "Disperse" — scatter words, ideas, and influence reflecting the Lord. Such a person adorns wisdom, making it honored and admired. How does the wise person use knowledge aright?

By sharing with others a knowledge of the Lord. Each person is a never-dying soul who will spend eternity somewhere. Then, logically, "He that winneth souls is wise" (11:30). In no other way can the lips be more wise or admirable. Words of warning are one sign of love. Suppose you should be in the pathway of a speeding train. Someone lustily shouts "Stop!" and saves you from your own carelessness. How valuable! How treasured! How appreciated! Surely a word in due season. Love prompts us to speak God's warnings to all who may be traveling toward spiritual destruction. This responsibility has always been enjoined (Ezek. 33:8,9). Those who hear and heed will be forever grateful.

A word of rebuke may be in due season. For instance, parental discipline. The right word at the right time can relieve a tense and unpleasant situation for everyone, including the child, preventing more difficulties later on. Words of discipline are never pleasant, but their fruit is sweet (13:24). A right use of knowledge from the Lord.

Words of faith to a doubting heart are indeed helpful. Forces on every hand are destroying faith in God, Christ, and the Bible. The world is hungering for stability for the present, hope for the future. Only an understanding of eternal values can provide these. So to erase one doubt and replace it with faith is truly a good word in due season. There is no greater need, no greater service.

Words in due season must be words of truth. To cry "peace," peace" when there is no peace shows a lack of wisdom and knowledge. To be blindly optimistic in spite of divine warnings is "out of season," and also out of harmony with common sense.

Christ spoke gracious words (Lk. 4:22) — sometimes gentle, sometimes harsh, sometimes rebuking, sometimes warning, sometimes commending and comforting, and always words of truth. All these can be "gracious words" when spoken "in due season." "A wholesome tongue is a tree of life" (15:4) — a vital, dynamic part of the good life. This is the possibility! Then surely, "The lips of knowledge are a precious jewel" (20:15).

FOR THOUGHT OR DISCUSSION

- Many sayings have been so often repeated that people tend to accept them as truth, failing to examine their validity. Among these is: "Sticks and stones may break my bones, but words can never harm me." Though words do not inflict physical harm, they can inflict heart-wounds much harder to bear than broken bones.

- Strife almost invariably begins with words. Then oftentimes pride prevents an honest settlement of the situation, a willingness to admit fault. Many are like the woman who said to her husband: "Well, I'll admit that I was wrong, if you'll admit that I was right."

- Profanity has become so common that many people cannot carry on a conversation without its use. Profanity exists in the heart. The word "profane" means to regard lightly or desecrate that which is sacred. For instance, Esau *profaned* his birthright (Heb. 12:16); he lightly esteemed that which was holy. So one who takes God's name in vain not only broadcasts the profane condition of his heart but violates a positive commandment (Ex. 20:7).

- Many years ago a Christian woman commented: "I am convinced that the devil invented the telephone." Why such a comment? She knew all too well how often the telephone is used to harm others with gossip. Of course, the telephone is no better or worse than the tongue behind it. Think how effectively the telephone *can be* used to spread a "good word."

- Concerning a woman known for her skill to start more fires with her tongue than others could extinguish, someone quipped: "When she dies, the mortician is surely going to have a big problem. Her tongue is so long that he will have a difficult time burying it." Does this perhaps involve too much truth to be very amusing?

Quotes to Consider

There is one excellency within the reach of everyone: brevity.

He who abuses others must not be particular about the answers he gets.

People who fly into a rage need their wings clipped.

If you would not have your enemy know your secret, tell it not to your friend. — Persian

Command your temper if you would command respect.

Birds are entangled by their feet, men by their tongues.

Govern your thoughts when alone, and your tongue when in company.

Meditate the language of the erudite, but do not speak it in the public square; there speak the language of the people, or else take refuge in silence.

A word unreasonably spoken may mar the course of a whole life. — Greek

No matter how right he may be, nobody loves the person who says, "I told you so."

Many a thing whispered in one ear is heard all over the whole town. — Danish

Rage is one weapon of a contentious person. What he lacks in logic he seeks to gain by anger.

Never part without loving words. They might be your last.

The unkind word falls easily from the tongue, but a coach with six horses cannot bring it back. — Chinese proverb

A wise man thinks all he says; a fool says all he thinks.

Egotism is an alphabet of one letter.

Thistles and thorns prick sore, but evil tongues prick more. — Danish proverb

Teach thy tongue to say: "I do not know." — The Talmud

If you are on the Gloomy Line,
Get a transfer.
If you're inclined to fret and pine,
Get a transfer.
Get off the track of doubt and gloom,
Get on the Sunshine Track — there's room —
Get a transfer.

If you're on the Worry Train,
Get a transfer.
You must not stay there and complain,
Get a transfer.
The Cheerful Cars are passing through,
And there's lots of room for you —
Get a transfer.

If you're on the Grouchy Track,
Get a transfer.
Just take a Happy Special back,
Get a transfer.
Jump on the train and pull the rope,
That lands you at the station Hope —
Get a transfer.

"She shall be praised."

7 — A Gracious Woman

A gracious woman. A charmingly appealing sound! Nearly all women would like to be so described. What image comes to your mind? Someone poised and pleasant? Well-versed in social graces? At ease under all circumstances? Admirable qualities, but graciousness includes much more. The dictionary defines gracious: "showing or bestowing goodness, kindness, or mercy; affable; polite." It literally means: "full of grace" and therefore involves spiritual qualities as well as charm and poise.

"A gracious woman retaineth honor" (11:16). Radiance emanates from her moral excellence, and she merits high esteem from God and man. "A virtuous woman who can find?" (31:10). "Virtuous" means "full of strength or power," denoting a moral force that is strong and far-reaching.

The climax of *Proverbs* is a detailed description of admirable and gracious womanhood, unsurpassed in sacred or secular literature. Let's look at the appealing picture given in Chapter 31.

A Gracious Woman Is Trustworthy

"The heart of her husband doth safely trust in her" (31:11) — unwavering confidence in all things. He can trust her to "do him good and not evil all the days of her life" (31:12) — ever concerned with his feelings, anxious to lighten his burdens and anxieties.

He can trust her with his love and loyalty, assured of her chastity, not doubtful or apprehensive of her conduct in his absence.

He can trust her with his good name. She will not criticize and parade his faults before others with words calculated to destroy respect for the very name which she also wears. Neither will she reproach his name by her conduct.

He can trust her with his possessions, knowing that she will use them wisely. Trust her with his credit cards? His check book? Confident that she will not overspend? Yes, of course. "He shall have no need of spoil" — no need to seek a soldier's spoil because of her extravagance or insistence on living above their means.

He can trust her with secret information, fully assured that it is locked forever in her heart, not to be shared with others. She does not abuse his confidence, but rather becomes more worthy of it as time goes by.

He can trust her with his children, knowing that she will care for them properly in his absence.

A Gracious Woman Is Industrious

"I wish I didn't have a thing to do today." Have you ever said this? Perhaps all of us have, thoughtlessly. But think. Many people don't have a thing to do today. Some are in hospitals. Some are in prison. Others, in poverty-stricken or war-torn nations, languish in the streets with no job, no home. Would we trade places with any of these? Of course not! We want to be an active, productive participant in society. This demands industry and responsibility.

To be "keepers at home" requires work. There's no escape from it. It is impossible to have a harmonious and smooth-running home if the woman in it is lazy. The gracious woman described in *Proverbs* accomplished so many tasks that it almost tires us just to read of her! She "worketh willingly with her hands" (31:13), so selfless that "she riseth while it is yet night, and giveth meat to her household" (31:15), and "eateth not the bread of idleness" — that is, bread not earned by work. "Her candle goeth not out by night" (31:18). How often has a light burned all night, as some woman cooled a fevered brow, comforted a distraught child, finished a garment or a meal, or supplied other needs for family and friends?

She "worketh willingly." This specifies the attitude: cheerfulness, not self-pity or martyrdom. Some women work hard, while constantly complaining of their responsibilities. The same tasks may be accomplished, but whether with a smile or frown makes a profound difference! Do we work *willingly?*

Gratitude determines attitude. Who would grumble about work to be done if she really feels: "I'm thankful for floors to sweep and beds to make. I'm thankful for a family healthy enough to be hungry. I'm thankful for health enough to care for their needs." Happiness does not consist of always doing what we enjoy, but rather in learning to enjoy what must be done. When you look at a stack of dirty dishes, what do you see? Some unknown writer expressed it like this:

> *Thank God for dirty dishes; they have a tale to tell;*
> *While others may go hungry, we're eating very well;*
> *With home, health and happiness, I shouldn't fuss;*
> *By the stack of evidence, God's been very good to us.*

Godliness does not cause a woman to downgrade household duties. Rather, it gives them real meaning and purpose. A broom, a mop, an iron, an oven. Unglamorous tools. But with them the gracious woman transforms the most humble tasks into a creative art. How? She creates a more comfortable and enjoyable life for her loved ones; and for herself, appreciation and the joy of usefulness. This puts a song in her heart, a smile on her lips, and changes seeming drudgery into a blessing. This cheerful outlook brightens the day for others, and adorns her with a beauty not found any other way.

She Guards Her Family's Welfare

The gracious woman "looketh well to the ways of her household" (31:27). This refers not to her house but household, or family. She is attentive not only to their physical needs but also to their spiritual welfare — their *"*ways.*"* She keeps close watch, sensing such dangers as bad habits, questionable companions, harmful activities, that which is watched on TV and studied in textbooks — ever alert to see whether any member of the household may wander or weaken.

Yes, a broom, a mop, an iron, an oven. *To these we must add a book, THE BOOK.* This is the gracious mother's tool by which she helps to mold eternal souls, creating a work of art which will outlive any statue chiseled from stone.

A Good Business Woman

The worthy woman manifested all attributes for business success, beginning with a willingness to work.

Business acumen led her to look for the best sources for her needs — "she bringeth her food from afar" (31:14). A bargain hunter? It seems that she spent thoughtfully and carefully.

Planning and organization. Understanding the value of time, she got up early and gave a "portion to her maidens" (31:15) — outlined their tasks for the day. Without planning, time can easily slip by with little accomplishment.

Foresight. She made preparation for the future. "She is not afraid of the snow for her household: for all her household are clothed with scarlet" (31:21). "Scarlet" refers not so much to color as to kind, meaning "double garments" or thick apparel to fortify against the cold, often woven in scarlet color for warmth. Realizing that winter would come, she provided for her family's needs in advance. She also bought a field for future use and security for her family (31:16). This included the principle of saving and investing.

Thrift. Without thrifty management of material assets, she could not have accumulated enough to buy a field.

She felt the pleasure of a task well done: "perceiveth that her merchandise is good" (31:18). She put her whole heart into her work, reaping the results of her energy and economy. To minimize and depreciate one's accomplishments, to feel no joy or pride in tasks well done, is neither commanded nor commended by God.

A Gracious Woman Must Have a Gracious Tongue

Energetic and clever organizers can become terse or even domineering, deficient in the gentler graces. Not so with the worthy woman. "In her tongue is the law of kindness" (31:26), words of sympathetic understanding. To strike a proper balance on many things is like walking a tight-rope. The truly gracious woman must learn to be:

Cheerful but not frivolous
Sober but not morbid
Firm but not harsh
Helpful but not meddling
Gentle but not compromising

And this is not easy! But then, becoming a gracious lady is not easy. Few ever attain it completely, and that very scarcity is one thing which fixes her value: "far above rubies." What a goal for which to strive!

A woman's words do so much to form the home atmosphere. A cheerful attitude and a good sense of humor work wonders. They help the entire family over the snags of daily living. Since words are the index to one's inner being, no woman can be called gracious unless she follows the principles discussed in Chapter 6. A self-willed and vexatious woman can make a home intolerable.

A Gracious Woman Is Chaste

Beauty and impurity are incongruous. Proverbs graphically describes the impure woman (6:24-29; 7:6-27). Her devilish wiles, her destiny, and the plight of her ensnared victims are discussed later.

"*As a jewel of gold in a swine's snout, so is a fair woman without discretion*" (11:22). Would a gold ring in a hog's nose beautify the animal's filth? Neither can a beautiful face make a lovely lady of one whose soul and body are desecrated with impurity. God admonishes older women to teach young women: "to be discreet, chaste, keepers at home, good" (Tit. 2:5). The woman who defies and rejects this lofty standard is a plague on society worse than death (Eccl. 7:26).

Realizing that her body is sacred, a godly woman guards her health. "She girdeth her loins with strength, and strengtheneth her arms" (31:17). She needs physical strength to enjoy all the wonderful things the Lord has in store for herself and the loved ones depending on her. Taking time for proper rest, diet, and exercise is not a mark of selfishness, but of unselfishness, if properly motivated and used.

A Gracious Woman Appreciates Beauty

An esthetic sense is God-given and makes the whole world lovelier and more enjoyable. God is the author of beauty. Wisdom's commendation of a "woman's touch" endorses a reasonable concern with the appearance of self, home, and family (31:21,22). A man once commented: "200 men can make a camp, but it takes a woman to make a home."

The primary importance of inward adorning in no way prohibits care of the exterior (I Pet. 3:4; I Tim. 2:9). Paying too little attention to personal dress and grooming, and to the home's orderliness and comfort, can result in much domestic unrest and contention.

A Gracious Woman Is Concerned About Others

She "stretcheth out her hands to the poor; yea, she reacheth forth her hands to the needy' (31:20). "The needy" — not only the cold and hungry, but the discouraged, bereaved, lonely, and ill, for the paramount needs are not material. Economic thrift plus liberality is a rare combination. It is easy to lean too far in one direction or the other, but her household thrift did not stop her ears to the cries of the needy.

This requires a heart of compassion, sensitivity to others' burdens, and enough unselfishness to spend and be spent — time, money, physical and emotional energy. The selfish and self-centered person can never merit the label of "gracious."

Is It Worth the Effort?

To strive toward this excellence is a lifetime job requiring hard work, determination, self-denial, and self-discipline. It cannot be achieved accidentally. Is it worth all the effort? What are the promised results and rewards?

A woman can, with God's help, transform herself into a

treasure more valuable, rare, and precious than all the world's wealth. "Her price is far above rubies" (31:10). Truly, a jewel unsurpassed. What a possibility! No material possession can begin to compare with the encouragement, help, and joy she brings to others. Therefore, we are not surprised to read:

"*Her children arise up, and called her blessed*" (31:28). During their early years, they may chaff at her discipline and question her judgment. But in later years she commands their respect and love, because they can look backward and know she served as both compass and anchor during their turbulent, uncertain years.

"*Her husband also, and he praiseth her.* Many daughters have done virtuously, but thou excellest them all" (31:28,29). Not every woman can be at the top of society's list, but most important for her is to be at the top of *his* list. How comforting and gratifying to hear your husband say: "You're the greatest woman in the world!" "A virtuous woman is a crown to her husband" (12:4) — that which adorns and elevates him also. No wonder he is proud of her!

"*She shall be praised.* Give her of the fruit of her hands; and let her own works praise her in the gates" (31:30,31). Not only by her children and husband, but she shall be praised by all who know her. "The fruit of her hands" — her whole life — bears testimony of her excellence. Therefore, if her name comes up where people are gathered, her praises are sung, justly and rightly so, for she is "adorned with good works" (I Tim. 2:10). "Her own works praise her." Though she loyally supports and reflects her husband's accomplishments, she is also recognized for her own achievements. The two are not contradictory but complementary.

A woman so loved, so admired, so praised! How is it achieved? "Favor is deceitful, and beauty is vain: but a woman that feareth the Lord, she shall be praised" (31:30).

"Favor [popularity] is deceitful." To center life around fickle human beings, what they may think or want us to do, will end in heartache. "Beauty [physical beauty] is vain." It avails absolutely nothing in the long run, for its destiny is the grave.

Then who is worthy of praise? "A woman that feareth the Lord." *Proverbs* begins and ends with this emphasis. Fear of the Lord is the only basis for excellence, real beauty and success. The praise and appreciation of husband and children herein described is indeed a much-to-be-desired treasure, but a woman's worth is not dependent upon others. Some of the world's most praise-worthy women, portrayed in both sacred and secular records, had neither husband nor children. But "a woman that feareth the Lord, she shall be praised," and she can be a "virtuous woman" whose value is "far above rubies" — a priceless and attainable goal for any woman!

FOR THOUGHT OR DISCUSSION

- A little boy was asked: "What is your favorite parable?" He replied: "The one about the multitude that loafs and fishes." Where do you think he got the idea that work is something to be avoided if possible?

- The woman portrayed in *Proverbs 31* had servants, so she labored not grudgingly or of necessity, but willingly. Evidently she understood that work is an honorable and necessary part of the contented life. She imposed nothing on her servants that she was not willing to do herself. One who is unwilling to serve is unqualified to command. A real lady is not afraid to soil her hands with the lowliest of needed tasks.

- The worthy woman planned the day for herself and her servants — not for her husband or his servants. Though careful with her tasks, she did not step outside her sphere of authority.

- "Whoso findeth a wife findeth a good thing" (18:22) — provided she is a good wife!

- Will the woman who looks well to the *ways* of her household, or family, allow them to partake of the glamorized garbage so prevalent on TV, movies, and video cassettes? Or will she be even more concerned about what goes into her family's minds than what goes into their bodies?

Quotes to Consider

To marry a woman for her beauty is like buying a house for its paint.

God hath often a great share in a little house.

The foolish and the dead alone never change their opinions. — Lowell

To the discontented person no chair is easy.

Time is money, but money is not time.

Mirth is the medicine of life; it cures its ills and calms its strife.

As the old birds sing, the young ones twitter. — German proverb

He that speaks of things that do not concern him, shall hear of things which do not please him. — Arabian proverb

Let prayer be the key of the morning and bolt of the evening. — M. Henry

---

'Tis the human touch in this world that counts,
   The touch of your hand and mine,
Which means far more to the fainting heart
   Than shelter and bread and wine;
For shelter is gone when the night is o'er,
   And bread lasts only a day,
But the touch of the hand and the sound of
   the voice
   Sing on in the soul always.

"A wise man is strong."

8 — A Strong Man

How lovely is a strong man! Women admire him and weaker men envy him. But who is strong? What is the measure of a man? Physical strength? Young men are prone to think so: "The glory of young men is their strength" (20:29). And surely the body is important. To misuse or neglect it is to desecrate one of God's noblest creations, but physical strength is not the measure of a man. Think of Samson. With immense physical strength, he was one of the world's most notable weaklings, weaving the web of his own destruction by his moral weakness.

The giants of the ages who wrote their names on history's pages possessed strength which had little or no bearing on physical qualities. Therefore, moral strength is more important, more powerful, and more to be desired than physical strength. Physical valor may come from brutal strength, but moral courage must come from character and therefore deserves more praise.

An unusually strong and skilled young athlete said his father told him repeatedly as he grew up: "Son, always remember that a real man is measured from his ears up, not from his ears down."

What is Wisdom's description of a strong man?

A Strong Man Desires to Learn

"A wise man is strong; yea, a man of knowledge increaseth strength" (24:5). In his much-quoted aphorism, Lord Bacon said: "Knowledge is power." However, Wisdom said this centuries ago. Increased knowledge enlarges the power to be, to do, to earn, and to influence. However, to be conscious of ignorance is the first principle of knowledge and success. Even Solomon recognized: "I am but a little child: I know not how to go out or come in" (I Ki. 3:7).

He who is worthy of being called a man, is unshaken in adversity, humble in prosperity, active and bold in danger; and, if he be not learned, has at least a love for learning.
—Ancient Proverb

First of all, a strong man listens to God. "The way of the Lord is strength to the upright" (10:29). Wisdom and strength are so inseparable that they are almost synonymous. Yet wisdom must come first. Strength is the result. Just think! By heeding Wisdom, a man has the privilege of linking himself to the Mighty One of the universe. No wonder he becomes strong!

"My son, be strong in the grace that is in Christ Jesus" (II Tim. 2:1). Through the Son, one appropriates the power of the Father. "Wherewithal shall a young man cleanse his way? by taking heed thereto according to thy word" (Psa. 119:9). A young man who follows God is far wiser and stronger than an older man who does not. A strong man takes the candle of the Lord to search his own heart, striving for spiritual excellence.

Therefore, a strong man is reverent. In some circles, contempt for all sacred things is regarded as a badge of intellectualism. Not so. Quite the contrary. The weakling spurns God's words and then fancies himself to be a man. The real man is wise enough to admit the power and authority of God, and this produces reverence. Every man is either building manhood or destroying it, depending on whether he is following His Maker's guidance.

A strong man learns from others. Only a fool thinks he has all the answers, no need to learn from anybody else. So the wise man is not afraid or ashamed to seek advice. Realizing that it is no disgrace to accept intellectual donations, he is willing to give his donors due credit and to share with them the honor of his achievements.

A strong man listens to his parents. "My son, hear the instruction of thy father, and forsake not the law of thy mother: for they shall be an ornament of grace unto thy head, and chains about thy neck" (1:8,9; 6:20). A man ceases to be a child, but he remains forever a son. So at any age, the respectful son honors his parents and returns their love. By this he glorifies God and adorns himself, for he is displaying one mark of true manhood which all the world can see.

The Strong Man Builds on Defeats

Defeat is a very real part of life, even for the righteous. No person succeeds at every task. One who does not understand this is likely to be overwhelmed with discouragement. One difference between a wise person and a foolish one is the ability to learn from mistakes, and from the mistakes of others. There is a vast difference between defeat and failure. To lose a battle does not mean we have lost the war.

How does the strong man handle the inevitable reverses? Wisdom gives such an encouraging example: "For a just man falleth seven times, and riseth up again" (24:16).

Though the falling may be caused by an enemy, the wise person doesn't even consider allowing the enemy to succeed. One of God's men of old issued a notice to his enemies: "Rejoice not against me, O mine enemy: when I fall, I shall arise" (Mic. 7:8). *Trials and reverses cannot overwhelm the wise person.* The key is simple: just don't stay down. The strong man resolves to get up one time more than he falls down. This leaves him the victor, no matter what or who caused the fall. So the wise person hopes for the best, is prepared for the worst, and makes the most of the present.

A Strong Man Has a Healthy Horror of Sin

Listening to God builds firm conviction. A wise man knows there is a vast difference between truth and error, right and wrong. "A prudent man foreseeth the evil, and hideth himself; but the simple pass on, and are punished" (27:12). A prudent man senses a situation which could possibly lure him into sin. What does he do? He literally runs from it. Hides from it. A weakling? A coward? Far from it! He is a smart man. A strong man. Fully aware of sin's consequences, he can foresee the end of a wrong road and make a right turn in time. He does not brand himself as a fool by making a "mock of sin" (14:9) or fancy himself to be a "good sport" because he is ready to follow others into mischief (10:23). There is a tendency today to condone, or even commend, people who do wrong; but God says:

> He that saith to the wicked, Thou art righteous; him shall the people curse, nations shall abhor him: but to them that rebuke him shall be a delight, and a good blessing shall come upon them (24:24,25).

"My son, if sinners entice thee, consent thou not ... walk not thou in the way with them; refrain thy foot from their path: for their feet run to evil" (1:10-19). This advice is not obsolete. It's just as relevant today as ever. Sinners love company. It isn't much fun to sin alone. Getting others to join them produces a sense of conquest, security, and approval. But a strong man is not afraid or ashamed to say "No," as discussed in Chapter 10.

A Strong Man Is Chaste, Holding Marriage in Honor

The sacredness of marriage was ordained in Eden and emphasized throughout God's Word. *Proverbs* affirms both the sacredness and joy of the marriage union (5:15-23), while condemning any violation: "Whoso committeth adultery with a woman lacketh understanding: and he that doeth it destroyeth his own soul" (6:32). So the person who ignores or violates this divine law of purity is not strong, but a weakling, because it is not smart to follow a course which destroys one's own soul!

The New Testament reaffirms: "Marriage is honorable in all, and the bed undefiled: but whoremongers and adulterers God will judge" (Heb. 13:4). The Creator makes no provision for a double standard, either before or after marriage, but requires the same purity for men and women.

A Strong Man Appreciates and Respects Noble Womanhood

All men should study Proverbs 31, the admonition of a mother to her son concerning women. Although priceless for women, it has valuable insights for men. It portrays the husband who was well aware of his wife's excellence, and he told her so! If someone had asked the virtuous woman: "Why are you willing to work your heart out day and night?" she might have answered: "One reason is that my husband appreciates me."

Praise is powerful! An ounce of praise is worth more than a ton of criticism. Wise is the man who understands this. One word of praise from a loved one often has the power to clean houses, cook meals, and prompt almost unbelievable achievements, for it furnishes compelling motivation.

> You may not sing in opera
> Or even write a book;
> But if you like the food you eat,
> Start braggin' on the cook!
> —Mary Oler

A Strong Man Is Kind and Compassionate

"That which maketh a man to be desired in his kindness" (19:22 ASV). Firmness to say "No" does not preclude kindness. The two are not incompatible, but harmonious. Kindness makes firmness more effective. Either without the other forms a warped being. Strength does not produce cruelty or formidable austerity. Christ confirmed this. He was firm and unmovable when any divine principle was challenged. Yet he was so kind that the weak, the sorrowing, the down-trodden, and little children were naturally drawn to him.

A strong man is tender-hearted and compassionate, sensitive to others' needs and feelings. Christ wept with his sorrowing friends. Paul wept over the ungodly living of some (Phil. 3:18). Tears are not a sign of weakness, but of strength and conviction.

A strong man is a gentleman — a gentle man. This produces the courtesy, refinement, and manners which "maketh a man to be desired." There is no substitute for refinement; neither wealth, knowledge, nor titles can take its place. King James I of England said: "I can make a man a lord, but only the Almighty can make a gentleman." "I have found that nothing is more useful to man than gentleness and affability" — Terence. Emerson said: "We sometimes meet an original gentleman who, if manners had not existed, would have invented them." Manners are mere kindness, courtesy, and consideration for others' feelings.

> Courtesy was born and had her name
> In princely halls;
> But her purest life may be the same
> In humble walls.
> —Ira Howard

Only weak characters are cruel. The successful person has a heart of mercy, not cruelty. By this he not only blesses others, but helps himself most of all. It's just the smart way to go! "The merciful man doeth good to his own soul; but he that is cruel troubleth his own flesh" (11:17). Definitely, a merciful kindness puts softness in the voice, takes wrangling out of the home, and oils society's friction-points. The strong and successful man knows this and is thereby motivated to show mercy to others, including the less fortunate (14:21) and even animals (12:10).

Attempting to settle controversies through physical violence is not the mark of a real man. Such never proves who is right, only who is stronger physically. A man who held different views from Aristotle once hit the philosopher and knocked him down. Aristotle got up, wiped the blood from his nose, and then said: "Now, my friend, let's proceed with the argument."

A Strong Man Obeys Civil Laws

"*My son, fear thou the Lord and the king*" (24:21). God has always endorsed government by law and obedience to civil powers (Rom. 13), unless such powers require citizens to disobey Him. The spirit of anarchy is contrary to every holy precept.

Another biblical principle is that the older shall govern the younger, not vice versa. If a young person has no respect for authority, age, or experience, and no gratitude for all things provided by preceding generations, he has forsaken everything which makes a man a man. "My son, fear thou the Lord and the king." This is real strength, a quality sorely needed by the young; for, all too soon, the mantle of responsibility will fall heavily upon their shoulders.

A Strong Man Is Responsible and Dependable

This involves industry and foresight. "He that gathereth in summer is a wise son" (10:5). A false idea has been popularized: that a mark of intelligence is to avoid work. However, the ability to accept a task, even an unpleasant one, and stay with it to completion is a sign of maturity and stability. God warns: "Meddle not with them that are given to change" (24:21). Through Jeremiah, God asks: "Why gaddest thou about so much to change thy way?" (Jer. 2:36). Unstable gad-abouts! This refers to spiritual instability.

However, success in every field requires responsibility, dependability, and maturity. The unpredictable gad-fly who flits irresponsibly from one task to another will in time wonder why he prospers less than others.

A Strong Man Has a Gracious Tongue

"*My son . . . my reins shall rejoice, when thy lips speak right things*" (23:15,16). "The words of a wise man's mouth are gracious; but the lips of a fool will swallow up himself" (Eccl. 10:12).

> Maintain your rank; vulgarity despise;
> To swear is neither brave, polite, nor wise.
> —Author Unknown

Christ spoke "gracious words" (Lk. 4:22). Few things are more disgusting than a man who erroneously thinks that profane or lascivious language is a mark of manhood. Rather, as emphasized throughout *Proverbs*, it is one mark of a fool! Therefore, a strong man avoids sins of the tongue and teaches his lips to speak graciously.

> Immodest words admit of no defense,
> For want of decency is want of sense.
> —Roscommon

A Strong Man Is Honest and Trustworthy

One tragedy of our time is that too many have accepted the premise that to con, to manipulate others to one's advantage, is one badge of superior intelligence. The strong man is smart enough to know this to be false, realizing that the manipulator loses in the long run. All of life's valuable relationships are built on trust: family relationships, friendships, business — so a wise man makes every sacrifice to protect his trustworthiness.

One who has shattered his own integrity harms himself most of all, but he also brings sorrow to all who associate with him. The Voice of Wisdom uses an interesting symbol: "Confidence in an unfaithful man in time of trouble is like a broken tooth, and a foot out of joint" (25:19). Disappointing, useless, painful, troublesome!

A Strong Man Is Beautiful in Age

"*The beauty of old men is the gray head*" (20: 29). How admirable is the man who has walked down the pathway of life, hand in hand with the Heavenly Father, leading his family in ways of righteousness. With the snows of many winters upon his head, he walks into the sunset at the close of his earthly pilgrimage, ready to meet the Guide who has led him along the way. Surely then "the hoary head is a crown of glory" (16:31).

How fortunate are children who have such a father! "The

just man walketh in his integrity: his children are blessed after him" (20:7).

FOR THOUGHT OR DISCUSSION

- For more than twenty-five years a business executive kept on his desk a plaque which stated: "Profanity is the effort of a weak mind to express itself." Needless to say, fellow employees, including other executives, found it rather easy to refrain from profanity in that man's presence! Surely, restraint is possible!

- Though a strong man is merciful and kind, the trend to associate cruelty and violence with masculinity is distressing and destructive. Cruelties once practiced by heathen nations, but abandoned by civilized people, are coming back in style! Violence and atrocities are not only graphically portrayed in the daily news but are now an integral part of much so-called entertainment! It is incredibly disturbing to realize that books are published to teach "how to express one's esthetic sense through torture!" Horror movies are favorites with many preteens. We must all work to combat these destructive trends and influences.

- Conscientious men feel the constant pressure of society's demands, family's expectations, and their responsibility to achieve what the world calls *success*. Don't you believe that many of them could feel an immediate sense of achievement, relief, and calm, IF they had a clearer understanding of what real success is?

- How important, then, for us to remember that "He that is greatest among you shall be your servant" (Matt. 23:11), and "Whosoever shall humble himself as this little child, the same is greatest in the kingdom of heaven" (Matt. 18:1-4).

- The inimitable Will Rogers once observed: "What this country needs is cleaner minds and dirtier fingernails."

- Man has been compared to a tree — it's only after he has been chopped down that his real maturity is revealed.

- A nationally-known athlete said that many of his teammates who claimed to be disbelievers would, when in a tight spot, utter half-way under their breath: "God help me." No matter how hard they try to stifle it, all people deeply sense a need for divine assistance.

Quotes to Consider

Talk of poverty! There is no poverty so pitiable as that of the man who has acres of land, but not an atom of love; whose riches rise into millions, but whose life sinks into insignificance.

Shrewdness, if bragged about, becomes a liability, for the shrewd are feared.

Superiority begets enemies unless it is tempered with modesty. A beautiful woman, if she be clever, dresses simply; a shrewd man is careful not to parade his wit in the presence of others less gifted.

No matter how often a fool has bitten into a worm, he continues to judge apples by their skin.

> O, blessed is that man of whom some
> soul can say:
> He was an inspiration along life's toilsome way,
> A well of sparkling water, a fountain
> flowing free,
> Forever like his Master in tenderest sympathy.

Bad men excuse their faults; good men leave them. — Ben Jonson

That man is to be feared who fears not God. — Turkish proverb

By others' faults wise men correct their own.

> Through this toilsome world, alas!
> Once and only once I pass;
> If a kindness I may show,
> If a good deed I may do
> To a suffering fellow man,
> Let me do it while I can.
> No delay, for it is plain
> I shall not pass this way again.

He that will not be counseled cannot be helped.

Small men hate; great men pity.

God helps the sailor but he must row.

Better go home and make a net than sit by the river wishing for fishes.
— Chinese proverb

> If youth knew what age would crave,
> It would both get and save.

He that hath learned to obey will know how to command. — Solon

The more a man knows, the more he is inclined to be modest. — Fielding

> Plough deep while sluggards sleep,
> And you will have corn to sell and keep.

Better a little with honor than much with shame.

Give me a good digestion, Lord, and also something to digest;
Give me a healthy body, Lord, and sense to keep it at its
  best.
Give me a healthy mind, good Lord, to keep the good and
  pure in sight;
Which, seeing sin, is not appalled, but finds a way
  to set it right.
Give me a mind that is not bound, that does not whimper,
  whine or sigh.
Don't let me worry overmuch about the fussy thing called I.
Give me a sense of humor, Lord; give me the grace to
  see a joke,
To get some happiness from life and pass it on to
  other folk.
    —Thomas H. Webb

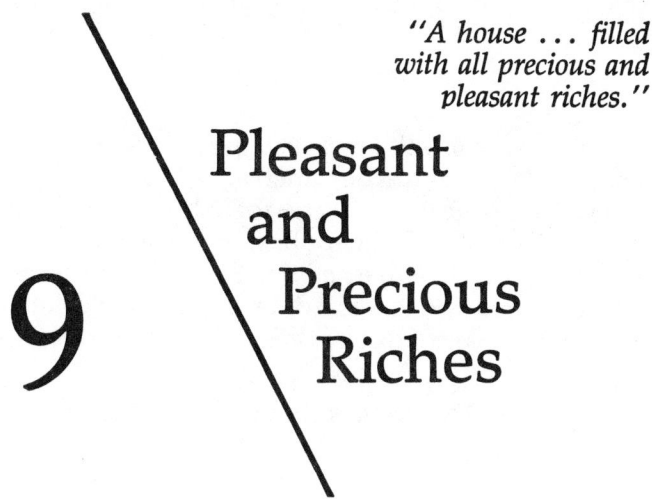

"A house ... filled with all precious and pleasant riches."

9 Pleasant and Precious Riches

Would you like to have a house filled with precious and pleasant riches? Such is a possibility. A meaningful and heart-stirring Scripture teaches:

Through wisdom is a house builded; and by understanding it is established; and by knowledge shall the chambers be filled with all precious and pleasant riches (24:3,4)

Does this mean expensive furnishings? Not at all. It has nothing to do with material possessions. "A house" — not brick or stone, but household or family. All of us are part of a family, regardless of present circumstances. "Chambers" of the house — the home relationships. "Wisdom, understanding, and knowledge" — the means by which every area of family life can be filled with wealth immeasurable.

Any complete success plan must necessarily include the home, for here so much time is spent. It is the heartbeat of all activities. Home attitudes and atmosphere permeate the whole of living, adding either comfort and security, or heartache and drudgery, to all other hours.

The Voice of Wisdom which guides the strong man and the gracious woman further instructs: "Every wise woman buildeth her house: but the foolish plucketh it down with her hands (14:1). This applies, of course, to men also. Few things, if any, remain static. Every home is being either strengthened and stabilized, or gradually plucked down and destroyed. Note some of these riches described in *Proverbs*.

The Riches of Love and Loyalty

In some homes, love reigns; in others, hatred. This fact is recognized: "Better is a dinner of herbs [meager fare] where love is, than a stalled ox [a feast] and hatred therewith" (15:17). Love sweetens the humblest way of life, while hatred negates the most luxurious surroundings. Today there are millions of restless, depressed, and discouraged souls walking around in expensively-clothed bodies, "boarding" in lavishly-furnished houses.

To be loved is a distinct and pervasive need. If this longing is not fulfilled at home, it may be sought elsewhere. What is love? It is a desire and willingness to seek another's best interest, even above our own. Love is not silent. Love manifests itself, but its absence speaks loudest of all. Words and actions are conspicuous and unmistakable indicators of the heart's feelings. Love — or lack of it — is hard to hide from spouse, parent, child, sibling, or friend. The beauty and value of a satisfying home life is probably most keenly understood by those who lack it. J. Paul Getty, one of the world's richest men, author of several success books, and many times married, said: "I would give my fortune for one happy marriage." So all who have a happy home life are richer than a billionaire who lacks this fortune — a fact often overlooked!

Loyalty is an essential part of love. A pie without cherries is *not* a cherry pie, no matter how loudly one may proclaim it so! Likewise, any relationship — whether with God or with each other — is *not* love if it is devoid of loyalty, no matter how loudly one may proclaim it so! This does not preclude seeing each other's faults. It means that we love enough to help correct faults, privately, not before the whole world. A child who is taught family loyalty is indeed blessed.

The Riches of Rest and Peace

The world is filled with confusion and unrest. God designed the home as a haven of rest and peace for body and spirit, where all can withdraw from outside pressures and fortify themselves for future tasks. Yet, contention — not peace — fills all too many homes. Home should be a place where all can relax, be themselves, freely expressing their innermost feelings; but bickering and strife can turn a house into a den of misery. Wisdom advises: "Better is a dry morsel and quietness, than a house full of sacrifices with strife" (17:1). A sumptuous feast may be good, but it satisfies only the body. An atmosphere of love and peace is necessary to feed the deeper hungers of the spirit. Therefore, the sorrow of discord in a home far outweighs the joy of material affluence. Hearts are far more touched by people than by things. The quarrelsome mother or father may work hard to provide every luxury, while robbing children of a treasure far more valuable: a peaceful home. Wise parents will solve their differences in private, as far as possible, thereby enhancing their children's feelings of security, peace, and family unity.

The Voice of Wisdom realistically describes a contentious woman, but surely the principles apply to any family member. "A continual dropping in a very rainy day and a contentious woman are alike" (27:15). — like a leaky faucet which drives the hearer to distraction! It is possible through constant urging to win an argument and by that seeming victory to harm or destroy love, respect, or friendship. Delilah did (Judg. 16:16,17). She won her battle and lost the war. One who fills the house with taunts, accusations, criticisms, harsh or ungodly words, is actually plucking down his or her own house. "It is better to dwell in a corner of the housetop, than with a brawling woman in a wide house" (21:9). The most humble place, even one of solitude or inconvenience, is preferable to a palatial house filled with a contentious person (and a contentious person can surely "fill" any house to overflowing!)

A peaceful home is not an accident, but an achievement requiring deliberate effort. To "follow after the things which make for peace" (Rom. 14:19) is not optional, but necessary, for abundant living. What will promote peace?

• Everyone in the home must desire peace, realize its value, and work to attain it. One person who loves to quarrel can disrupt the entire household and cause indescribable grief.

• Practice of the Golden Rule is a major factor (Matt. 7:12). Christ's admonition to put ourselves in others' place and treat them as we would be treated cannot be improved or over-emphasized.

• We should be tolerant and forgiving. Though disagreements naturally arise, these can be weathered for "Love covereth all sins" (10:12). That is, love is tolerant, understanding, forgiving. Home is where we are inclined to be our least attractive selves, so how often we need love to cover our weaknesses. Should we ask more than we are willing to give? (See Matt. 7:3).

• Each person must watch his tongue. Unless we follow the principles covered in Chapter 6, no peace can prevail.

One cause of contention is a failure to accept the God-ordained authority and duties inherent in the parent/child, husband /wife relationships. Strife is inevitable if any family member rejects or ignores these basic principles. Authority must be recognized. No person is exempt, for even the father must submit to the authority of God. And specific responsibilities are enjoined on each.

Another major cause of strife is a family's failure to live within their means. One key to contentment is a very simple principle: to work to decrease our wants. "There is treasure to be desired and oil in the dwelling of the wise; but a foolish man spendeth it up" (21:20). The wise family establishes a rule, honored by every member: to *spend less* than they *make*. This brings an honorable and peaceful dignity to any home, no matter how humble. This is easier if we just relax and remember always that if we had all the world's wealth, it would not bring happiness or contentment.

Too many families suffer from dislocated priorities which can be corrected by applying the therapy outlined in Matthew 6:33. So the order of priorities for the wise family's budget is: first, a scriptural portion to the Lord's work; second, a planned savings investment for the inevitable "rainy day;" and, then, they live on what is left, no matter how many sacrifices are required. This demands self-discipline; but it avoids the nerve-shattering pressure of debts, and the necessity of imposing on others when emergencies arise. Truly one mark of wisdom!

The Riches of Parental Guidance

Nothing is as helpless as a human infant. A little bit of cuddly, adorable flesh, housing an eternal soul. Who is to nurture this tiny body and spirit? God gave this exalted privilege and responsibility to parents. What is involved? *Providing physical needs,* and the parent who refuses to do this is worse than an infidel (I Tim. 5:8). *Providing spiritual needs* includes authority, love, teaching, and training.

Authority is essential for peace, order, and accomplishment in any institution. Can you imagine a bank, school, or business without any recognized authority or chain of command? The home is not a democracy where each has equal voice, though surely each deserves a sympathetic ear at all times. However, the Lord has enjoined specific duties upon fathers (Eph. 6:4) and both parents have responsibilities in the realm of authority (6:20-23).

Love is a spiritual need. Without assurance of being loved, a child is likely to develop all kinds of emotional problems. God recognized this need, admonishing aged women to teach younger women to "love their children" (Tit. 2:3-5). Doesn't every parent love his or her child? Obviously not, or this instruction would be unnecessary.

Training is an important spiritual need (22:6). To train a tender growing vine upon a trellis, both nourishment and corrective guidance are required. If this guidance is too harsh, the plant will be broken. With no guidance, the vine becomes unruly and unsightly. With proper guidance and care, it flourishes in radiant beauty for all to admire. So it is with a child who must be nourished with love and instruction; but without discipline, or corrective guidance, a child grows unruly and unsightly and never reaches his loftiest potential. Thus, training involves these necessary ingredients: teaching, discipline, and example. And a truism should be recognized: in order to train children at home, it is necessary for parents and children to spend some time there — together!

• Teaching right principles has always been enjoined upon parents (Deut. 6:6-9; Eph. 6:4). A young mind will absorb something. It is not a vacuum. If not filled with correct precepts, it will embrace wrong ones. Seed sown into minds during formative years determine what people become. Lord Byron, English poet and well-known libertine, wrote:

> The thorns that I have reap'd are of the tree I planted;
> They have torn me, and I bleed.

I should have known what fruit would spring from such a seed.

Today, thorns tear our nation and our families — and we bleed! Why? One unalterable law of God is that reaping is a direct result of sowing. So if we don't like the harvest, we must change the sowing. This demands careful examination of *all seed* being sown into the minds of the young, at home and elsewhere.

• Parental discipline is a special kind of love, commanded by God, for "Foolishness is bound up in the heart of a child; but the rod of correction shall drive it far from him" (22:15). The "rod of correction" is to promote the child's spiritual growth (23:13,14). Failure to do so shows a lack of love: "He that spareth his rod hateth his son: but he that loveth him chasteneth him betimes" (13:24). "Betimes" — at times, not continuously but occasionally as need arises. Too frequent correction, either verbal or physical, defeats the intended purpose. "Chasten thy son while there is hope, and let not thy soul spare for his crying" (19:18) — before it is too late. The timing is very important. A little discipline early in life can prevent the necessity for more severe correction or punishment later on.

However, to spare the rod, to let the child have his or her own way, is easier. No normal parent enjoys inflicting punishment on an offspring. The proverbial truth: "This hurts me worse than it does you" is understood by every loving parent, though not by the child. Nevertheless, to spare the rod is cruel. Why? The undisciplined person never learns self-control. Then he or she becomes an unruly child, a wayward youth, and a disillusioned, unhappy, and maladjusted adult. He grows up believing that all the world should stand aside and let him have his own way. When this does not happen, he does not know how to cope with himself or his surroundings, confirming that "he that spareth his rod hateth his son." It is the child who suffers a lifetime, caused by the parents' neglect to obey the Lord's child-rearing instructions.

- Example is by far the most effective teacher. "Telling" is not synonymous with teaching or training. Character is both taught and caught. A parent who says one thing and practices the opposite should never be surprised when children go astray. Of course, it is not possible for parents to be perfect, but children can easily perceive whether a parent is trying to live consistently right.

The Riches of Filial Honor and Respect

To "honor thy father and thy mother" specifies no age limit. This enriching aspect of home life begins the day we are born and never ends. Even after parents are gone, our lives continue either to honor or dishonor them. A child is responsible for his conduct, for "even a child is known by his doings, whether his work be pure, and whether it be right" (20:11).

In formative years honor is exemplified by obedience, which has always been enjoined: "A wise son heareth his father's instructions, but a scorner heareth not rebuke" (13:1; 19:26; 20:20; 6:20). Penalties for disobedience have always been severe (Lev. 20:9 — a Scripture quoted in Matt. 15:4).

The abundant harvest reaped from obedience should surely furnish strong motivation to heed wisdom's advice in this area of happy home life.

- Our parents are responsible for our lives. Who can ever measure the prayers, sacrifices, sleepless hours, anxiety, and hard work of godly parents? To despise such is inexcusable ingratitude. Children not fortunate enough to have righteous parents (and there are many!) should resolve more fervently than ever to live in a way to merit honor and gratitude from their own children some day.

- Parents are God's appointed agents to see the mistakes of children and mold their lives aright. In most cases, other people have neither the love nor the opportunity to do so. With all censure and no praise, a child feels discouraged, inferior, and defeated. On the other hand, all praise and no censure causes an exaggerated and distorted picture of one's own virtues. Either extreme produces an unhappy and maladjusted adult unable to fit into society's expectations and responsibilities.

• Parents are a child's first contact with authority, a life-long and ever-present aspect of living. The submissive child reaps big dividends throughout life. A merchant placed an ad in the paper: "Needed for employment: a boy who obeys his parents." If a child is permitted to disobey parents, is he or she likely to obey the authority of God, government, teachers, employer, or any other? To allow such rebellion is a serious injustice to any child. Disobedience to parents is listed among the most grievous sins (Rom. 1:30; II Tim. 3:2). It is not a trivial matter, left to the option of parent or child. Parents who allow it contribute to the child's sin.

• A rebellious, ungrateful child is one of life's sharpest sorrows and disappointments. "He that begetteth a fool doeth it to his sorrow ... a grief to his father, and bitterness to her that bare him" (17:21,25). Nothing makes a child despicable more quickly than an unruly, rebellious attitude toward parents. It is ugly and repulsive. It dishonors God, dismays parents, and disgusts others, causing them to avoid the child if possible. Children who shun responsibility are a source of shame and heartache to parents (10:5).

• On the other hand, the obedient child is an honor to God, a joy to parents, and adorns self with life-long blessings which are "... an ornament of grace unto thy head, and chains about thy neck" (1:9). "A wise son maketh a glad father; but a foolish man despiseth his mother" (15:20). A child can be one of life's most satisfying joys! "Children's children are the crown of old men" (17:6).

• One pressing need today is for parents and children

to study Wisdom's admonitions diligently. The child's entire future is at stake. So is the future of all society.
Honoring parents does not end with childhood. This honor includes supplying parental needs, always endorsed by God. It is a serious matter. "If any provide not for his own, and specially for those of his own house, he hath denied the faith, and is worse than an infidel ... If any man or woman that believeth have widows, let them relieve them, and let not the church be charged; that it may relieve them that are widows indeed" (I Tim. 5:8, 16).

FOR THOUGHT OR DISCUSSION

- The home is the God-ordained training ground for the successful life. If children are not taught morals, manners, consideration for others, unselfishness, respect for authority, and the priority of spiritual values, they become immoral, inconsiderate, selfish adults unprepared to cope with social, material, and spiritual responsibilities. These are the truly under-privileged children!

- Many young parents were strongly influenced by Dr. Benjamin Spock, popular author on child-rearing, who advocated extreme permissiveness. After witnessing the fruit of such teaching, he later admitted publicly that "too much permissiveness doesn't work." Of course, parents who reared their children according to Solomon, not Spock, knew this all the time.

- Some secular psychologists today teach that the home is a democracy where each has equal voice. A totally anti-biblical teaching. Surely each person's views should be heard and considered, but any institution which does not have some recognized center of authority cannot long operate harmoniously, if at all. This principle is recognized in God's organization of the family.

- A talented lady made a very attractive plaque to hang in their home: "May this house be filled with all precious and pleasant riches."

- The popular movie "Love Story" — highly influential among young people — contained a line frequently repeated: "Love means never having to say you're sorry." Nothing could be more false or antibiblical! Few stop to think that this is an atheistic concept. The movie's major characters were portraying atheists, married in an atheistic ceremony. The truth is: love means a constant readiness to say we're sorry.

Quotes to Consider

We ought to weigh well what we can only once decide. — Cyrus

Evil conduct is the root of misery. — Chinese proverb

He labors in vain who tries to please everybody. — Latin proverb

> Politeness is to do and say
> The kindest thing in the kindest way

If you would lift me, you must be on higher ground. — Emerson

Economy is too late at the bottom of the purse. — Seneca

To live according to one's means is honorable; not to do so is dishonorable.

> This for the day of life I ask:
> Some all-absorbing, useful task;
> And when 'tis wholly, truly done,
> A tranquil rest at set of sun.

Courage consists not in hazarding without fear, but in being resolute-minded in a just cause.

Don't promise what you cannot perform — Turkish proverb

There is no piety in keeping an unjust promise.

> It takes two to have a quarrel,
> But only one to start it.

He that can read and meditate will not find his evenings long or life tedious.

> What matter will it be, O mortal man,
> when thou art dying,
> Whether upon a throne or on the bare
> earth thou art lying?
> —from the Persian

There is no greater misfortune than not to be able to bear misfortunes. — Latin proverb

Money is a good servant but a bad master. — French proverb

He who sows courtesy reaps friendship, and he who plants kindness gathers love.

Who chastises his child will be honored by him; who chastises him not will be ashamed.

Better the child cry than the old man.

Discipline is a medicine to be used sparingly lest its virtue be lost.

What is learned in the cradle lasts to the grave.

Unless the clay be well-pounded, no pitcher can be made.

A father loves his children in hating their faults.

> Worry and Fret were two little men
> That knocked at my door again and again.
> "O pray let us in, but to tarry a night,
> And we will be off with the dawning of light."
> At last, moved to pity, I opened the door
> To shelter these travelers, hungry and poor;
> But when on the morrow I bade them "Adieu,"
> They said, quite unmoved, "We'll tarry with you."
> And, deaf to entreaty and callous to threat,
> These troublesome guests abide with me yet.

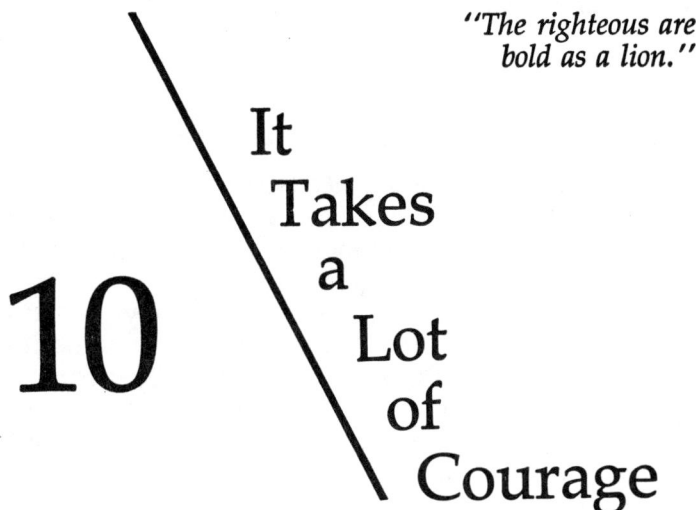

"*The righteous are bold as a lion.*"

10 It Takes a Lot of Courage

If someone rushed into a burning building to save a life, we'd say: "What courage!" And surely that's right. The dictionary defines courage: "bravery; boldness; fearlessness; that quality of spirit which faces danger without flinching." An admirable and desirable trait. Courage in physical feats is commendable. However, living a righteous life requires more unflinching courage than anything else in the world. It cannot be done by weaklings or cowards! Think of the symbolism used:

"*The righteous are bold as a lion*" (28:1). It takes bravery to stand for truth when it's popular to fall for anything, when the world's "intellectuals" say that the Bible is only a myth and that righteousness is only for the weak and ignorant. But following the Lord increases boldness and assurance: "I will never leave thee, nor forsake thee. So that we may boldly say, The Lord is my helper, and I will not fear what man shall do unto me" (Heb. 13:5,6). What an exalted privilege! The Power of the Universe is a Helper of the righteous. This is the basis of courage to cope with cares, responsibilities, problems, persecutions, and temptations.

The Certainty of Temptation

Temptation confronts us daily. Satan dangles his bait before us in countless and varying forms. It may be a lure to sins of disposition, sins of the tongue, sins of neglect and apathy, sins of the flesh, discouragement, or a wavering faith. On and on goes the list. Some lures are easily recognizable. Others are subtly disguised, oftentimes so smoothly and attractively that the real danger is undetected until the devilish work is accomplished. To understand that this battle is inevitable is the first step. The next step is to resolve that we can and must, with the Lord's help, have the courage to be victorious.

All are tempted, but temptation is not sin. Some people mistakenly equate the two, believing that being tempted is just as bad as committing the deed. Some even quip: "It's just as bad to think something as to do it." Is this true? Of course not! Though it is surely possible to sin in thought, this prevalent idea is false. How do we know? Temptation always involves thought. Christ was "in all points tempted like as we are, yet without sin" (Heb. 4:15). He thought, and he was tempted, but he didn't yield. Refusing to follow through on the thought, he cast it from his mind and resisted. Because he experienced temptation, he sympathizes with us.

God does not require the impossible. Therefore, it is possible to develop the courage to follow Christ's example. Think of this reassuring promise:

> *There hath no temptation taken you but such as is common to man: but God is faithful, who will not suffer you to be tempted above that ye are able; but will with the temptation also make a way of escape, that ye may be able to bear it (I Cor. 10:13).*

Courage to Go Against the Crowd

Anybody can go along with the crowd. No courage is required. But the smart person asks where the crowd is going. True grit is required to go against the majority, to be on the unpopular side, to be called "different," "square," "goody-goody" by those who lack the courage to do right.

It took courage for Daniel to worship God in the midst of a heathen nation, to endure the horror of the lions' den. A little boy described Daniel: "Part of him was backbone, and the rest of him was grit."

It took courage for Noah to endure the ridicule, laughter, and taunts; but he continued to hammer, saw, build, and preach, reaping the rewards of righteousness.

Many people today, men and women, have a strong tendency to regard sinful conduct as hilariously funny, the "in" thing, something of which to boast, one mark of a "good sport," a sign of sophistication calculated to elevate the sinner in the eyes of peers. This is not new, but an ancient concept which brands a person a fool. "Fools make a mock at sin" (14:9). "It is a sport to a fool to do mischief" (10:23).

Righteous people have always been in the minority. "Thou shalt not follow a multitude to do evil" (Ex. 23:2) — and evil is what the multitude will always be doing. How do we know? Christ warns that most people walk the broad way which leads to destruction, while few walk the narrow way that leads to eternal life (Matt. 7:13,14). So if "everybody else is doing it," we must be doubly wary and cautious. We have a choice and the glorious privilege of walking with the few, the real victors!

Think: how valuable is soup without a bowl? How valuable is a life which recognizes no boundaries, no restrictions? So how wonderfully comforting to know that our Father has outlined the boundaries necessary for the happy, productive, fulfilled life. The wise person observes these boundaries, gratefully.

Courage to Say "No" to Strong Drink

"Be not among winebibbers" (23:20). Christ's law condemns drunkenness and warns that it will destroy the soul (Gal. 5:21), but only *Proverbs* paints a realistic picture of what strong drink will do to body, mind, and soul. The detailed description is amazingly accurate and up-to-date.

Strong drink is deceptive, making promises of joy and relief which it is powerless to fulfill (20:1).

Strong drink is destructive, causing "Woe ... sorrow ... contentions ... babblings ... wounds without cause ... and redness of eyes," leading to other sins (23:29-33) and resulting in a tortured and turbulent spirit from which there is no relief or escape (23:34,35). So Wisdom says to all: "Be good to yourself. Avoid all these woes by avoiding their cause — strong drink."

Today, alcohol is the most widely-used of all destructive drugs, being responsible for more than half of all fatal automobile accidents, the primary killer of teens. Alcohol destroys bodies, minds, marriages, peace, and souls. Of course, other modern mind-altering drugs come under the same warning and condemnation. How urgently needed is the courage to listen to Wisdom's advice!

Courage to Resist the "Strange Woman"

Women's power to lead men into sin has been evident from the beginning. Someone has quipped that Adam's downfall was not the fruit on the tree but the "peach" on the ground. The lure of designing women is forcefully emphasized in *Proverbs*. Surely Solomon was familiar with feminine wiles! And God used him to warn men of every generation. It is as though he pleads repeatedly: "My son, my son, heed my words. Don't fall into the moral pits as I did."

Purity is specifically commanded in the New Testament, but *Proverbs* furnishes the most masterfully realistic picture in all literature of the manner and method of the "strange woman" — a term applied to any woman not lawfully one's own according to God's precepts (7:5-27).

A description is given of the woman. She made no secret of her intentions, but advertised them by her manner of dress (7:10) and by the places she frequented (7:12). Her method is outlined. Step by step, she lured an unsuspecting young man into her web, as a spider charms and lures a fly.

- She made an appeal to his conscience, seeking to silence it and lull it to sleep. In effect, she said: "Don't worry. I've made my offerings to God, so everything's all right" (7:14).

- Next, she appealed to his ego, one of the strongest of all motivating forces. With flattering words, a kiss, and an impudent look, she made him think he was extra special (7:5, 13, 15).

- Then, she appealed to his natural inclination for physical pleasure (7:16-18).

- She convinced him they were safe from detection (7:19,20).

- With "her much fair speech" and "flattering of her lips she forced him" (7:21). Not physical force, but her combined arsenal of weapons was more powerful than his moral strength. He finally succumbed to her design and intent.

A description of the young man is also given. He is called "simple" — that is, unlearned and inexperienced. Not that he lacked intelligence, but he had no understanding of the fatal trap he was entering. Do you suppose the young man thought he was "simple?" Surely not. He may have thought the entire episode was his idea! Most likely he fancied himself to be exceptionally sophisticated and mature. Actually, he was as an ox going to slaughter, as a fool going to the stocks, and as a bird going into a trap (7:21-23).

The result: the young man was "slain" — not physically but spiritually. He followed the lure down the perfumed velvet pathway to hell and death (7:24-27) as many before him — men who thought they were strong, but they were unaware of the fatal entanglement. The woman's destiny was also spiritual death: "Her house is the way to hell, going down to the chambers of death."

Other detailed descriptions of the "strange woman's" strategy are given in 2:16-22; 5:1-14; 5: 20-23; 6:20-35. These very practical admonitions apply to all, of course, for God does not endorse a double standard of conduct.

Who Is a "Smart Bird?"

The young man who yielded to sin is described "as a bird hasteth to the snare, and knoweth not that it is for his life" (7:23). It takes a smart and strong person to recognize a trap and avoid it. If a bird should recognize a trap, he would be stupid to fly into it to his own destruction. So is the person who is lured into wrongdoing. He walks into a trap and triggers his own doom. Any stupid weakling can do it. The real "chicken" is one who follows the other "fouls." The "smart bird" flies out of range of those who would shoot him down.

There is no merit or achievement in being like jello — conforming to any mold dictated by surrounding circumstances and people. This forfeits our own priceless privilege of decision-making. So: "If sinners entice thee, consent thou not" (1:10). That's smart!

To allow others to lead us into sin is a mark of stupidity. There is a story about a fox and a donkey who met on the bank of a frozen river. "They tell me," said the fox, "that you are speedy on land but helpless on ice." "Is that so?"

snorted the donkey. "Let's race across the river and I'll show you." They started across the frozen river, but the fox stayed well behind. Suddenly the donkey shrieked in fright: "The ice is too thin. It's breaking under me, and I'm sinking." "That's what I wanted to find out," said the fox as he smugly trotted away, leaving the donkey to perish in his own ego and folly.

How To Be a "Smart Bird"

Can a wise person fortify against temptation, learning to recognize a sin-trap in time to avoid it? Indeed, but the preparation must be made in advance.

The "smart bird" *resolves to follow the Father's will at all costs*. Transgression of divine law is a sin against God, as well as our own souls. Joseph resisted Potiphar's wife, saying: "How can I do this great evil and sin against God?" Joseph's resolve on this issue was fixed *before* his time of testing. Only firm spiritual conviction provides motivation for righteousness and resistance against sin.

The "smart bird" *uses the test of foresight and common sense*, examining what the conduct under question has done to others. Is the eventual result constructive or destructive? REMEMBER: every influence which touches you today is lodged deep within the recesses of your brain and remains a part of you *forever*.

The "smart bird" learns to recognize the tactics of Satan who is real, alive, diligent, persistent, smart, and determined (I Pet. 5:8). We are soldiers in a spiritual battle. Football teams study films of the opposing team. Why? To learn their strengths, weaknesses, and strategies. Shouldn't we be smart enough to study the strategy of our soul's enemy, and brave enough to resist him (Jas. 4:7)? Satan has an advantage, if we are ignorant of his devices (II Cor. 2:11). Gradually, with soft enducements, his evil work is wrought. Delilah conquered a man who had resisted all warriors.

Nobody becomes a profligate all at once; but with every yielding to temptation, the conscience becomes less sensitive. Sin deludes and then destroys. The tempter entices in gentle and subtle degrees; but the tempted must resist quickly and decisively, in one brave moment. Of course, it takes great courage! So we must be forewarned and forearmed for the inevitable conflict.

The "smart bird" avoids sin by avoiding temptation, when possible. Who knows in advance how much strength one may have, or lack? "Let him that thinketh he standeth take heed lest he fall" (I Cor. 10:12). Therefore, the wise person strives:

• To avoid things which prompt evil thoughts — whether a conversation, a book, a magazine, TV, or a movie "for mature audiences." Familiarity with sin can destroy abhorrence of it. Nobody lives in a vacuum. Therefore, the most effective way to combat evil is to crowd it out with wholesome and constructive thoughts and activities.

• To avoid close association with people known to engage in that which is wrong or questionable. REMEMBER: *Satan works through people!*

• To avoid places where temptation is certain or likely.

The "smart bird" counts the cost. Sin is enjoyable (Heb. 11:25) — but it's not free! The cost is high, and the "smart bird" looks at the price tag before swallowing Satan's sales pitch. One of his most powerful "lines" is to convince people that they can enjoy the pleasures of sin without reaping the consequences. Such was his appeal to Eve and to every human being since that time.

No principle is more important to understand than this one: though we are free to choose our *conduct,* it is impossible to choose the *consequences.* Adam and Eve could choose to eat the forbidden fruit, but they were powerless to choose the consequences of their choice. Anyone can choose to sin, but sin has its price: the inescapable consequences (Num.

32:23; Gal. 6:7,8; I Tim. 5:24). The cost is high. Too high! Truly, "the way of transgressors is hard" (13:15). So no wonder Wisdom pleads with us to walk in the Lord's way. It's for our good, for our happiness.

Courage Day by Day

Discouragement is one of Satan's most powerful weapons. It simply means loss of courage. It takes great courage to discharge daily responsibilities — when perhaps nobody knows or seems to care — and to battle the pressures from all sides without bending or breaking. Yet this home-grown, garden-variety of courage is often overlooked or minimized. Our Heavenly Father is keenly aware, however. After He had assigned Joshua the gigantic task of conquering the land of promise, He bolstered his confidence by telling him repeatedly: "Be of good courage."

It takes a lot of courage to admit mistakes and sins, whether large or small. Pride and ego often stand in the way. Few people exhibit the courage and humility of David who said: "I have sinned." Simple everyday relationships could be so much smoother and more enjoyable if each person had the courage and humility to say freely: "I was wrong about that. I should not have done or said so-and-so. Please forgive me."

A Profile of Courage

Yes, it takes a lot of courage. One supreme example is the apostle Paul, one of the world's most educated and influential men.

He had the courage to break with the religion of his early training, and leave his position among the intellectually elite, to embrace and disseminate the simple gospel of Christ.

He had the courage to endure indescribable hardships and persecutions (II Cor. 11:23-28) and the heartache of false brethren.

He had the courage to live a pure life (I Cor. 9:27). *He had the courage, in the presence of royalty, to defend the gospel* with such power that King Agrippa admitted: "Almost thou persuadest me to be a Christian" (Acts 26:28). *Paul's ultimate courage was shown as he faced death,* not for crimes, but for defending truth. We hear these ringing words of victory: "I have fought a good fight, I have finished my course, I have kept the faith" (II Tim. 4:7). Courage is a fighting quality. Cowards accept error, but the brave defend truth. Christianity is a battle between right and wrong. We are called to "put on the whole armor of God" and fight courageously as the "Captain of our salvation" commands.

FOR THOUGHT OR DISCUSSION

- Courage is contagious. Barak said to Deborah: "If you will go with me, I will go." Deborah went and courage flowed from her to Barak and on to 10,000 soldiers and the victory was won.

- Satan has popularized some powerful false clichés, such as: "Anything is permissible between consenting adults." Joseph knew this to be false when he resisted his boss's wife. David knew this to be false when he realized his sin with Bathsheba.

- Other false clichés: "Anything goes as long as it doesn't harm anyone else." "Victimless crimes should not be punished." There is no such thing as a "victimless crime" or a sin that "doesn't harm." If nothing more, sin always leaves pain and scars in the heart of the sinner: guilt, remorse, loss of self-respect — until eventually sin hardens the heart, silences the conscience, and renders the sinner incapable of repentance. Then the soul is hopelessly lost, destroyed by the slow suicide of sin.

- Just as smashing the barometer does not avert an approaching storm, so ignoring the gravity of sin does not prevent the inescapable consequences.

- From the time of Adam, people have tried in vain to repeal the law of sowing and reaping. One aspect of this unalterable law is usually overlooked: the reaping is always more abundant than the sowing, whether good or evil.

- God's children are not required to live as though they had no body — but with the soul in control of the body.

- Someone quipped to this writer: "So you're writing about Solomon, the man who loved women." My reply: "No. Solomon didn't love women. He used women. To go to a different tent each night is no evidence of love, but rather disproves it. Having many women (even a thousand!) is no compliment or achievement of which to boast, as even the aging Solomon himself realized. It takes far more ability, character, and love to understand and build a mutually fulfilling relationship with one woman."

- Someone wisely observed: "The devil entangles youth with beauty, the miser with gold, the ambitious with power, and the learned with false doctrine."

Quotes to Consider

O for a man to rise in me,
That the man that I am
May cease to be.
— Alfred Tennyson

Build a little fence of trust
   Around today;
Fill the space with loving deeds,
   And therein stay.
Look not through the sheltering bars
   Upon tomorrow;
God will help thee bear what comes
   Of joy or sorrow.
—Mary Frances Butts

Grief halted at my door,
"My burden's great, and I'm footsore,"
Said he.
"Then come thou in!"
I cried.
"The supper's spread —
The sweet rye bread."
Grief put his burden down,
And stepped inside,
And, parting, left a gift with me —
The world-wide gift of Sympathy.
    —R. C. Sheffield

Be with me, Lord, where'er my path may lead;
Fulfill thy word, supply my every need;
Help me to live each day more close to thee.
And O, dear Lord, I pray abide with me.

And better had they ne'er been born
Who read to doubt or read to scorn.
    —Walter Scott (concerning the Bible)

Be like the bird that, halting in her flight
Awhile on boughs too slight,
Feels them give way beneath her and yet sings —
Knowing that she hath wings.
    —Victor Hugo

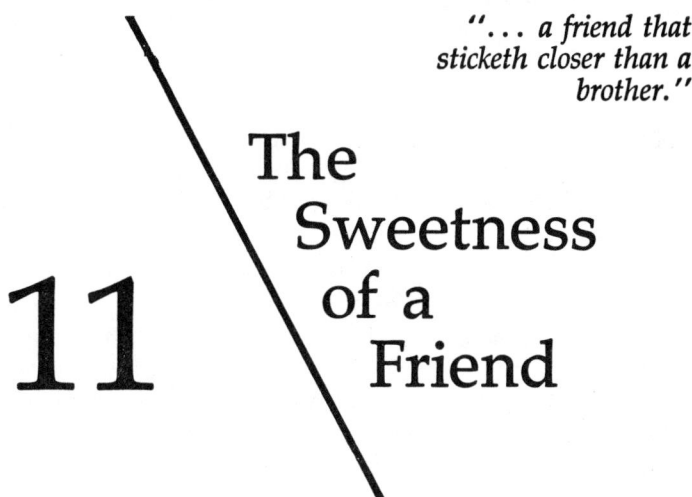

"... a friend that sticketh closer than a brother."

11 The Sweetness of a Friend

True friendship is one of life's most treasured blessings. A good friend is like an old shoe or a faithful dog — comforting, heart-warming, reassuring. The writer of *Proverbs* describes this relationship in a unique, thought-provoking way: "Ointment and perfume rejoice the heart; so doth the sweetness of a man's friend by hearty counsel" (27:9). Ointment and perfume were lavished upon honored guests as a gesture of courtesy and concern. Surely such treatment gladdened the guest's heart. So does the sweetness of a friend's words.

In a special way, friendship involves the most difficult and delicate art of dealing with others. However, the rewards are so priceless that all should strive to develop the skill, and *Proverbs* furnishes many necessary guidelines.

The Powerful Influence of Friends

The Voice of Wisdom uses interesting and intriguing symbolism: "Iron sharpeneth iron; so doth a man sharpeneth the countenance of his friend" (27:17). When a knife is sharpened against iron, the interaction influences both instruments. So does friend influence friend. It's inevitable. The influence is so powerful that even the strongest cannot fail to absorb some of the ideals, disposition, morals, language, and goals of frequent associates. We influence all we touch. All we touch influences us, far more forcefully than we usually realize. Why?

Companionship is so dear that we are naturally inclined to please our favored associates. When a devoted friend says, "Come, let us do this or that," the pull is tremendous. It takes immense strength to size up all the consequences and make an on-the-spot decision to say "No" when we should.

We do not fully know our own weaknesses. This is verified by thousands who have fallen in their fight with sin, even though they thought they were strong enough to stand. Such was true of Peter. He weakened and allowed others to influence him to deny his Lord.

We do not fully understand Satan's determination to lead us into sin! and this is most effectively done through those we love. We are warned that evil companions corrupt good morals. Therefore, to shun the company of some is not cowardly or unkind. It's smart! This being true, great caution should be used in forming friendships.

Wisdom's Guidelines for Choosing Friends

"He that walketh with wise men shall be wise: but a companion of fools shall be destroyed" (13:20). Associating with wise people will increase our wisdom as the influence blends. *"Go from the presence of a foolish man, when thou perceivest not in him the lips of knowledge"* (14:7). To become the companion of fools can pull life downward to destruction. But who is a fool? According to Wisdom's definition: one who does not regard God and his law. Therefore, we should be continually conscious of the importance of cultivating friends among those who strive to

live according to divine guidelines — having values which impact constructively, not destructively, on the relationship. *"Make no friendship with an angry man; and with a furious man thou shalt not go."* Why? "Lest thou learn his ways, and get a snare to thy soul" (22:24,25). There are some people with whom we can never have a peaceful or congenial relationship. It is wise to be with them as little as possible, for a close association could actually cost our souls. We cannot attain our highest possibilities with those whose ideals clash violently with our own. Paul and Barnabas experienced this. Though both were good men, their thinking so differed that they deemed it wise to part. Separately, each did a good work. How much greater the conflict would have been if one had been "an angry man."

It is not wise to attempt to buy friendship, favors, or position. "A man's gift maketh room for him, and bringeth him before great men" (18:16). "Wealth maketh many friends ... and every man is a friend to him that giveth gifts" (19:4-6). This does not make a recommendation. It merely states a fact. A person of wealth can easily gather many "friends" who shower him or her with flattery as payment on their own social insurance. This creates an illusion of friendship and security. Yet, in reflective moments, the wealthy person may wonder or doubt if he is truly loved for himself alone, never knowing for sure until the testing time comes. When wealth flees, so do some "friends." Job experienced this. So it is not wise to try to win friends by wealth.

Wisdom warns not to become obligated to evil people. "It is not good to accept the person of the wicked" (18:5). "Eat thou not the bread of him that hath an evil eye, neither desire his dainty meats" (23:6,7). Some have been unsuspectingly led into trouble because they accepted favors. Suppose an unrighteous benefactor should help you get a job or aid your child significantly. Such a person may have a scintillating personality, concern for others, popularity, social status, and wealth — characteristics which tend to enhance influence and obscure vices. If such a benefactor should ask you to participate in his or her worldly lifestyle, what should the answer be? Naturally, the temptation would be to rationalize that gratitude demands a reciprocal relationship; but read again Wisdom's admonition given above.

Young people who are dating are choosing friends who will influence their entire lives, and perhaps their eternal destiny. How alert and super-sensitive they should be to these guidelines given by our Heavenly Father. It is wise to ask: "Will this person help me go to heaven?" If not, is any friendship (or marriage) worth losing one's soul? The stakes are too high. So the wise young person chooses friends with extreme care and thoughtfulness. Remember a simple truism too often overlooked: you marry someone you date. So it is not reasonable to date a person who has no regard for God's law, because you just might marry that person; and if so, you have lessened your chances for a happy marriage and a satisfying family life.

On Being a Friend

Friendships are so cherished that we should strive to keep them in good repair. Love is a living thing, and any living thing can be killed. The love of friend for friend must be nurtured. If we concentrate on *being* a friend, *having* friends will take care of itself. After all, we cannot control the actions of others. We can determine only our own conduct. How can we enhance friendship?

To love is a part of friendship. "A friend loveth at all times" (17:17) — not a constant display of affection, but a tender and indestructible concern under all circumstances. Love is best defined: to seek another's best interest. True love or friendship is not shaken by prosperity, or the adversity of sickness, sorrow, discouragement, poverty, or dishonor. It's easy for some people to stand by friends when they are down, because this engenders in them a feeling of superiority. The real test is passed by those who remain faithful when friends pass them on the way up the ladder of success, whether material or non-material accomplishments. This confirms love, free of envy, for "love envieth not" (I Cor. 13:4). Others are good "friends" during prosperity; but when adversity hovers near, they simply don't have time to be bothered.

Being trustworthy and truthful will preserve friendship. "Confidence in an unfaithful man in time of trouble is like a broken tooth, and a foot out of joint" (25:19). A friend who proves unfaithful in time of trouble is not only disappointing but useless. "A brother is born for adversity" (17:17). A friend is one who has faith in us even when we lose faith in ourselves, so we should encourage our friends in a special way when their self-confidence needs a boost.

Be friendly. "A man that hath friends must show himself friendly" (18:24). When you meet someone, what is uppermost in your mind? How he or she is treating you? Or how you are treating that person? To concentrate on making others feel at ease and appreciated will strengthen all associations.

Don't take slights too easily. "He that covereth a transgression seeketh love" (17:9). Love causes us to look tolerantly upon friends' faults, even words which should not have been spoken. Most likely, no offense was intended. It is much better to show a magnanimous spirit by letting the matter rest. Some wise person advised: "Throw little things over your shoulder, rather than carry them as a load on your chest."

Make every effort not to offend. "A brother offended is harder to be won than a strong city" (18:19). Of course, if the brother is a true friend, he will forgive the offense, but to prevent conflict is far more pleasant for everybody. This eliminates the pain of trying to cure it. These verses show the necessity of a give-and-take attitude. We want others to overlook our foolish errors. How often we need understanding! Therefore, we should exercise the same tolerance we request. Discuss differences, if any, in private. "Debate thy cause with thy neighbor himself; and discover not a secret to another" (25:9).

Don't criticize or downgrade friends in their absence. This weakens confidence, for listeners realize that the speaker would also criticize them in their absence. Remember: there is always a "little bird" to carry the message, and then a friend may be lost. Solomon warned: "A bird of the air shall carry the voice, and that which hath wings shall tell the matter" (Eccl. 10:20).

Don't get too close. As already mentioned, the influence of friends on each other is as "iron sharpeneth iron" — but the irony of it is that it can grow too sharp and wear too thin! Wisdom warns of this danger: "Withdraw thy foot from thy neighbor's house, lest he be weary of thee, and so hate thee" (25:17). The context of this Scripture teaches moderation in all things. "Hast thou found honey? eat so much as is sufficient for thee, lest thou be filled therewith, and vomit it" (25:16). That which is beneficial, sweet, and pleasurable in moderation becomes nauseating in excess. Many treasured friendships have been smothered to death. As our grandmothers warned: "Don't wear your welcome out." Ancient secular proverbs also advise:

A little more than enough is much too much.

Visiting your neighbor is no crime; but your visits should not be so often repeated, as to induce him to say, It is enough.

Don't encourage friends to reveal confidential information. This is kin to the previous thought. We should provide a listening ear when needed, but never a prying tongue. Encouraging others to reveal personal problems is fraught with danger. Such has destroyed many meaningful relationships. Why? Later, when the troubled friend is less irritated with those involved (whether family member, or others) he or she is likely to despise himself or herself for revealing more than discretion warranted. This causes a feeling of uneasiness around those who shared the moments of anger or weakness. Especially, no friend should be goaded into saying things about a spouse which may be later regretted in calmer and more thoughtful moments.

Don't betray confidences. If someone comes to us with a heavy heart and entrusts a secret, it is not ours to spread. It is actually the property of another, a treasure left in our care. To betray that trust can result in losing a friend and in destroying others' relationships. "A whisperer separateth chief friends" (16:28). "He that repeateth a matter separateth very friends" (17:9). A good friend is a good listener, but not a good repeater.

Don't try to tend to a friend's business. This can easily cross the border of concern and become meddling. When people are close, it often becomes easy to be too free with advice. Advice is seldom welcome, even when solicited. Unsolicited, it is usually resented. It is easy to drift into the habit of saying: "Why don't you do this or that?" In effect, this is attempting to make others' decisions for them, if they have not requested such suggestions.

The Joys and Benefits of Friendship

Ah, how good it feels!
The hand of an old friend.
—Longfellow

True friendship is a spiritual communion founded on mutual esteem and respect for certain standards, a blending of two spirits with like loves, ideals, and aims, complementing each other's moral and social needs. "As in water face answereth to face, so the heart of man to man" (27:19). Just as surely as a face reflects itself in the water, true friends are sensitive to each other's needs. Being like-spirited, one heart answers to another.

> Friends are each other's mirrors, and should be
> Clearer than crystal, or the mountain springs,
> And free from clouds, design, or flattery.
> —Catherine Phillips

This spiritual unity can be stronger than blood-ties. Wisdom advises that under some circumstances it is better not to "go into thy brother's house in the day of calamity" but rather to rely on that "neighbor that is near" — the friend who has stood firmly by in prosperity and adversity (27:10). There is a "friend that sticketh closer than a brother" (18:24). We choose our friends, not our relatives. But how wonderful it is when our relatives are also our friends!

An approving, encouraging, cheerful, or loving look can do so much to lift the heart. It can speak volumes without a word. "The light of the eyes rejoiceth the heart" (15:30). Eyes have been called the windows of the soul. Through them we can see so much of one's inner being. For this reason, just one look often has the power to cause a heart to soar or to sink. With just one look, Christ said so much to Peter that he went out and wept bitterly (Lk. 22:61,62). How powerful those same eyes must have been to comfort, to cheer, to instill faith and confidence. When Jeremiah was sent to preach to a sinful nation, he was admonished: "Be not afraid of their faces: for I am with thee to deliver thee, said the Lord" (Jer. 1:8). Countenances — looks, eyes, expression — speak so loudly to instill doubt and discouragement, or courage and comfort, in the heart of others. What do our *looks* say?

"The hearty counsel" of a friend can be so reassuring. Often-

times we are doubtful of our own decisions, needing guidance from those who love us. This "hearty counsel" may at times include correction. "Faithful are the wounds of a friend" (27:6). "Open rebuke is better than hidden love" (27:5). It is better to rebuke in love than to hide disapproval when correction is needed; but we must be as quick to receive a rebuke as to administer one, and all reproof should be done in private. An Arabian proverb says: "Advice given in the midst of a crowd is loathsome."

A real friend is rare and priceless. The standard is high, both in being a friend and in having one. Is this standard ever met? Yes, but not frequently. A wise counselor said: "If you have, at the close of your life, enough real friends to count on one hand, consider yourself very fortunate. Few people do." Some people live and die without understanding this, for they never experience enough severe crises to winnow their friends from their acquaintances. The very scarcity of friendship is one element of its pricelessness.

> Those friends thou hast, and their adoption tried,
> Grapple them to thy soul with hooks of steel.
> —Shakespeare

FOR THOUGHT OR DISCUSSION

- What about the countenance of our friends when they leave our presence? Have they been "sharpened" with good? with optimism? with elevating thoughts! or with gossip? with destructive thoughts? What about the countenances of our families as they leave the house each morning?

- We are in a certain family by chance, being born or adopted into it. But our friends are by choice. If our families had a choice, would they choose us as a friend?

- Since close friendships are so powerful and important, we can see God's wisdom in providing for Christian fellowship in the church, where those who are like-minded may find the friendship which the heart craves. Yet, not all church members do right, and it may at times be necessary to shun the association of some whose influence would be destructive rather than constructive.

- In an article titled *If I Were Twenty-One,* James L. Gordon makes so many excellent points, including the following:

    If I were twenty-one again I would have two or three choice friends among older people. They know the way. They have learned the meaning of life. They can be depended upon in the hour of emergency. They have traveled over the same road. They yearn for the compliment of your confidence. They would like to be of service to you. They would like to count you among their few favorites. They would like to be of assistance to you in your plans and schemes. They would glory in your success and boast among their friends of your achievements. Cultivate the friendship of the folks who are older.

Quotes to Consider

Friendship multiplies joys and divides griefs.

To preserve a friend three things are required: to honor him present, praise him absent, and assist him in his necessities. — Italian proverb

True friendship is a plant of slow growth. — Washington

So live with thy friend that if he become thine enemy he can do thee no harm. — Tully

A friend is one to whom we may pour out all the contents of our heart, chaff and grain together, knowing that the gentlest of hands will take and sift it, keep what is worth keeping, and, with a breath of kindness, blow the rest away. — Arabian proverb

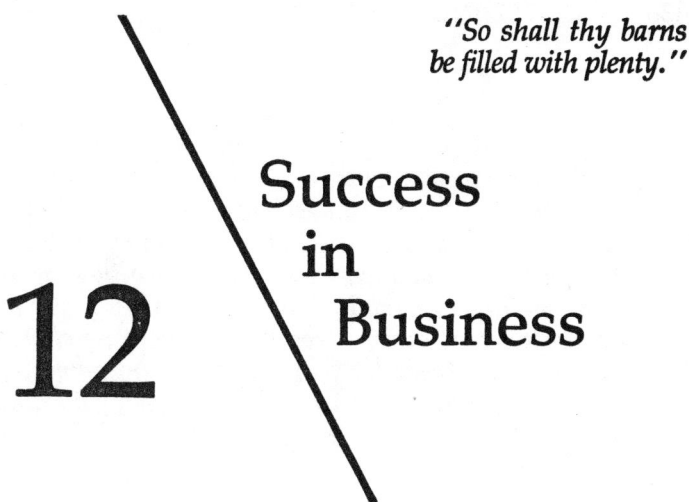

12 Success in Business

"So shall thy barns be filled with plenty."

Economic success is on the minds of millions each day. Some merely wish for it. Others work for it. Some succeed. Others fail. The Lord has more to say about it than many have supposed. Economic responsibilities are part of the Christian life. From the time a child learns to ask for money for a candy bar, each person sustains a lifetime responsibility and relationship to the acquisition and use of material things.

Some try to divorce material achievements and spiritual values. This is impossible, impractical, and unchristian. Guidelines of our Creator regulate both, so blended that they cannot be separated.

Poverty is not dishonorable unless caused by laziness or extravagance. On the other hand, there is no inherent virtue in poverty, as some have supposed. Lazarus was not righteous *because* he was poor, and the rich man was not evil *because* he was rich (Lk. 16:20-25). In his book, *Success*, O. S. Marden gives a thought-provoking admonition:

I wish I could fill every young man who reads these pages with an utter dread and horror of poverty. I wish I could make you to feel its shame, its constraint, its bitterness, that you would make vows against it ... *Praise it who will, poverty is narrow, belittling, contracting; there is little hope in it, little prospect in it, little joy in it; it is a terrible strain upon the affections, and often kills love between those who would otherwise live happily. It is the duty of every young man and woman to exert every nerve to get out of its clutches into freedom where the individuality can find untrammeled expansion* ... *Poverty is a curse* ... *and those who extol its virtues are the last to accept its conditions.*

Wealth can be a strong fortress, when properly gained and used. God gives the manual for economic success — how to get out of poverty's clutches, to have "barns filled with plenty" (3:10).

Temptations and pitfalls accompany both poverty and wealth (30:8,9). Either can be a snare to the soul, so our task is to learn our responsibilities.

The Right Attitude

Economic success begins with an attitude. The problem of materialism is ever-present. Its solution is not isolation or rejection of material things. Rather, the answer must be in our attitude toward their acquisition and use.

We must be willing to do our part. To think that financial success depends on God — that we pray, sit, and wait for it — is to deny our responsibility and freedom of will. On the other hand, to assume that all things depend on us is to deny divine Providence and aid. Both are essential. Someone has aptly observed that we should pray as though everything depends on God, and work as though everything depends on us.

God should come first with our possessions. Since He is the giver of all wealth, we should gladly "Honor the Lord with thy substance and with the *firstfruits* of thine increase; so shall thy barns be filled with plenty and thy presses shall burst out with new wine" (3:9,10). Notice the condition which precedes the result. The Lord even challenges us to put this to a test (Mal. 3:10). However, no blessing is promised the one who gives merely as an economic investment, for the "sacrifices of the wicked are an abomination" (15:8). An attempt to bribe God, thinking that He will multiply the stipend and return it to us, is a despicable motive. God has never endorsed "slot machine" religion.

If we would prosper, we should maintain the right attitude toward the wealth of others. Envy must be eliminated (14:30). The Christian who despises and condemns the financial triumphs of others should not expect the Lord to bless him with the very success that he loathes and criticizes in his fellowman! One tragedy of envy and covetousness is that these distressing traits not only keep people from enjoying what they have but drain the energy which could be used for worthwhile accomplishments.

A Willingness to Work

A business executive has this motto on his desk for all employees to see:

> If your future is hazy
> Could be you're lazy

All wealth is dependent upon work — either one's own or someone else's. The lazy person who refuses to work is actually a thief, dishonestly living on the labors of others, taking that which he did not earn. Therefore, laziness is immoral. In pungent words God condemns it and endorses industry, in both material and spiritual endeavors. The extent to which laziness can paralyze all achievement is graphically described:

The slothful man saith, There is a lion in the way: a lion is in the streets. As the door turneth upon his hinges, so doth the slothful upon his bed. The slothful hideth his hand in his bosom; it grieveth him to bring it again to his mouth. The sluggard is wiser in his own conceit than seven men that can render a reason (26:13-16).

The lazy person is always full of excuses and explanations for his lethargy. And no excuse is too far-fetched! "There is a lion without, I shall be slain in the streets" (22:13). How unlikely and ridiculous! The lazy person thinks he is so smart ("wise in his own conceit")! After all, isn't he getting out of a lot of work? One who is looking for an excuse can find it and convince himself that it is valid.

"The sluggard will not plough by reason of the cold; therefore shall he beg in harvest, and have nothing" (20:4). He complains: "It's too cold. I just don't want to work." Then he has no harvest and resorts to begging from those who endured all discomfort and ploughed in the cold.

"The way of a slothful man is a hedge of thorns" (15:19). Difficulties, either real or imagined, can always stop him from working. "I don't feel well." "It won't do any good." "When I married, my husband promised to care for me, so why should I have to work like a slave?" "I'm worth more than I'm paid. If my employer can't see my real worth, I'll just quit." "It's beneath my dignity to work for what they offered; I'd rather just draw an unemployment check."

Laziness had been defined as voluntary inertia. It is the parent of want and misfortune. "The soul of the sluggard desireth and hath nothing: but the soul of the diligent shall be made fat" (13:4). A wish without exertion is useless.

Those who talk and fail to toil will sooner or later wake up and wonder why they prosper less than their fellows. "In all labour there is profit: but the talk of the lips tendeth only to penury" (14:23). Employees who talk, talk, talk — consuming time and avoiding work — usually wonder why they are passed over at promotion time. They never realize that perhaps they used their tongue to reduce the size of their paycheck. Others have the mistaken idea that with a fraudulently slick tongue they can advance themselves to riches. Of course, this Scripture does not forbid the proper "talk of the lips," which is a necessary part of many honorable professions. Conscientious labor, whether mental or physical, is commendable and profitable.

Laziness is a road that goes downward. "I went by the field of the slothful ... it was all grown over with thorns ... so shall thy poverty come ... as an armed man" (24:30-34). Laziness caused neglect. Then neglect brought poverty. The man had a field, yet became poor. Why? By failing to use what he had. Yet the lazy person is usually surprised when poverty comes. It seems sudden, and he is likely to ask: "What happened? What robbed me of the things I want?" Actually, poverty came gradually, but the victim either could not or would not recognize his or her own laziness as the actual robber.

The lazy person is a source of irritation to an employer (10:26).

God decrees that one who will not work forfeits the right to any material blessing, even food (II Thess. 3:10).

The Importance of Thrift

Careful and frugal use of what we have is essential. It is more difficult to manage money than to make it. "He becometh poor that dealeth with a slack hand: but the hand of the diligent maketh rich" (10:4). This is not to be confused with stinginess or covetousness. Thrift is refusing to waste; stinginess is refusing to share. Thrift is preserving what we have; covetousness is wanting what the other person has.

Christ taught thrift. He had power to create unlimited amounts of food, but he instructed that the left-overs be saved (Jno. 6:5-13). One mother follows this example and then prepares what she calls "glamorized specialties." It's amazing how left-overs can be palatably disguised! She had learned the art.

Thrift in all things equals an increase in income, for it is surely true that a dollar saved is a dollar earned. A peaceful dignity pervades any home that is living within its means, no matter how humbly. It's better to live on less and avoid the pressure of unpaid bills (17:1). To live above one's means brings on far more problems than it solves. What is gained? Neighbors impressed? Our own disillusioned idea that we have attained? On the other hand, what is lost? Peace of mind? Family peace? Are some even tempted to dishonesty? So families who adopt the policy of spending less than they earn take a giant step toward a home filled with contentment and unshattered nerves. A very important aspect of the fulfilled life!

An ancient proverb admonishes: "Live not on credit, and you shall live in liberty." Our grandmothers had a motto which has never been improved:

> Eat it up
> Wear it out
> Make it do
> Do without

The Importance of Saving

Saving is necessary for prosperity in business. "There is a treasure to be desired and oil in the dwelling of the wise; but a foolish man spendeth it up" (21:20). Controlling wants is essential. One who spends all he makes this week can never enlarge his business next week. This is exemplified by the worthy woman who "considereth a field, and buyeth it" (31:16). Without foresight and self-discipline to spend less than she made, she never could have bought the field. The wise person has enough maturity to forego today's wants in view of tomorrow's needs.

To invest savings in view of future growth is a principle approved by Christ (Matt. 25:14-20).

Saving is necessary to meet future needs. Severe financial reverses can come at any time. Also, time may decrease our earning power. God gave us the ability to anticipate these possibilities. "Dig a well before you are thirsty" — suggests a Chinese proverb. Yet, during prosperity many live in reckless self-indulgence, with no self-discipline or restraint, later becoming objects of charity whose burdens must be borne by provident people. To live like the "grasshopper" and then expect the "ants" to care for us violates every divine precept.

The Matter of Timing

Timing is important. Many have willingly labored hard and yet hindered themselves financially by improper timing. For instance, a crop must be planted and harvested at the right time. If done too early or too late, all labor and profit can be lost. Proper timing is based on both foresight and dependability. Without dependability, one has little chance of succeeding in any field. The merchant who opens his store at 8:16 one morning and 10:44 the next may soon wonder where his customers have gone. They probably went to a dependable competitor. The salesman an hour late for an appointment may find his client has lost all interest.

Developing forethought, discernment, self-discipline, and dependability indeed brings rich rewards in all of life's pursuits.

According to Ability

Successful work must be according to ability and suitability. The five-talent man or woman should not be held to the pace of one talent. Such would kill initiative and reduce life to dull regimentation. Jesus did not so teach. On the other hand, the one-talent man who refuses to recognize his limitations, while looking with envy and bitterness at the five-talent man, will dwarf his own accomplishments and destroy his peace of mind.

Set realistic goals. The oft-repeated cliche "You can do *anything*, with enough determination" is false. Though determination is a virtue and a necessary ingredient for success, it alone is not sufficient. Striving for impossible goals — goals for which a person may lack ability or suitability — has resulted in disillusionment and despair for many. To recognize our inabilities is not self-depreciating but wise. Everybody has strengths and weaknesses. Lions cannot climb trees. If they could, nothing in the forest would be safe. But who has ever doubted the strength, power, and value of this king of the jungle?

"Go to the Ant"

The ant is a marvel of creation, mentioned twice in the Bible and described as exceedingly wise. We are admonished to heed her example (6:6-8; 30:25). These Scriptures summarize and confirm the principles just discussed. "Go to the ant, thou sluggard; consider her ways, and be wise." What ways? Ways of intelligence, industry, and foresight.

Intelligence. If an elephant were proportionately as intelligent as an ant, can you visualize what would happen? Of course, the ant works by instinct, not reason; but her instinct was instilled by the Creator who gave us intelligence and reason. So intelligence should prompt us to do what the ant does by instinct. If not, surely the Lord would not have commended her ways to us.

Industry. Note the characteristics of the ant's work:
- She works in spite of inconvenient or uncomfortable circumstances, in summer heat.

- She works in spite of uncertainty, never knowing when a foot may crush and destroy all fruits of her labor. If so, she rebuilds.
- She works with patience and steadfastness, never giving up in discouragement.
- She cooperates and works with others, all sharing in the total accomplishments.
- She is not afraid to tackle seemingly impossible tasks. Have you ever watched her struggle with a load many times her size?
- She uses her burden as a stepping-stone — at times placing her cargo across a crevice, then walking on it to the other side.
- She works willingly, not compelled from without, but impelled from within. How much more should Christians, motivated from within, labor to provide for self and others.
- She works when it needs to be done. Suppose she should spend most of the summer lying on the husks inside her home, telling herself; "I'll go to work in a little while." Procrastination could cause her to be unprepared for the winter.

Foresight is also exemplified by the ant. Preparedness. She stores up provisions for the time when circumstances will halt her labors. Foresight is essential in both material and spiritual success.

In a Nutshell

Daily we deal with material things. There is no escape. The God-ordained principles herein discussed apply to everyone: housewife, student, "white collar" worker, "blue collar" worker, professional, or entrepreneur. All have the duty and privilege of earning and /or using money wisely.

In light of fore-going Scriptures, this may be summarized. We should:
- Work hard and make all we can honestly.
- Give to God scripturally.
- Manage thriftily.
- Save thoughtfully.
- Understand always the relative value of spiritual riches and material riches.
- And never forget that every good gift comes from above (Jas. 1:17) so we should thank God constantly for all blessings.

FOR THOUGHT OR DISCUSSION

God made all things for our enjoyment (I Tim. 6:17), but we must beware of wealth that costs too much! When is the price too high? When it causes the loss of things money can't buy.

- *Losing one's soul to gain a fortune is indeed a bad bargain.* "For what shall it profit a man if he shall gain the whole world and lose his own soul?" (Mk. 8:36). Gradually and imperceptively, the love and pressure of possessions can crowd out spiritual priorities (Matt. 6:33) and lead people completely away from God. Indeed, a price too high.

- *Wealth gained dishonestly costs too much.* Dishonesty, though lightly regarded by many, is an abomination to God (see Chapter 5). Greed and desire for a quick and easy dollar leads to all kinds of evil (28:20-22), even to violence and murder (1:10-16).

- *Wealth can increase temptations and opportunities for sinful pleasures,* leading some into moral traps from which they never extricate themselves. If so, surely the price is too high!

- *To forfeit peace of mind to gain a piece of gold* is also a price too high. One that is "greedy of gain troubleth his own house" (15:27). It can cause heartache or even dishonor to the whole family. "Better is a little with the fear of the Lord, than great treasure and trouble therewith" (15:16). "Trouble" — the anxiety attending increased wealth. If this crowds out life's loftier values, it's not good business.

- *Wealth is too expensive if it costs family associations.* The parent whose time, energy, and nerves are so consumed with material things that little is left for the family runs a risk of losing the most valuable riches. Children grow up and leave home. Age, sickness, or death can descend upon a companion. Then it's too late to go back and fill lost years with treasured hours of family association.

- *Losing a friend to gain a dollar,* or thousands, is indeed a bad bargain. Friendships are tested and may be broken over nothing more than a few dollars. Wealth that costs too much! too much!

- *Trusting in riches is foolish and destructive.* "He that trusteth in his riches shall fall" (11:28). Surrounded by comforts, it is easy to feel a false sense of security. Some live like the man who enjoyed an illusion of safety by locking himself in his 5 x 5 cabin on a sinking ship. Riches can so easily "make themselves wings" and "fly away as an eagle toward heaven" (23:4,5). It is certain that we will be separated from them before long, one way or another. So surely, wealth is the weakest of all anchors!

Quotes to Consider

Good name in man or woman
Is the immediate jewel of their soul.

Let honesty and industry be thy constant companions. — Franklin

A man of words and not of deeds
Is like a garden full of weeds.

Labor rids us of three evils: tediousness, vice and poverty. — French proverb

Learned fools are the greatest of all fools. — German proverb

Whatsoever thy hand findeth to do, do it with thy might. — Ecclesiastes 9:10

No honest man ever repented of his honesty.

Beware of little expenses; a small leak will sink a great ship. — Franklin

Fidelity bought with money is overcome with money. — Seneca

'Tis not what we have but what we enjoy that makes us happy.

Idleness is the rust of the soul.

Ask your purse what thou shouldst buy. — Scottish proverb

Never give up! it is wiser and better
   Always to hope than once to despair;
Fling off the load of Doubt's cankering
      fetter,
   And break the dark spell of tyrannical
      care;
Never give up, or the burden may sink
      you —
   Providence kindly has mingled the
      cup;
And in all trials and troubles bethink
      you
   The watchword of life must be —
      Never give up.

"His children shall have a place of refuge."

13 A Place of Refuge

What heart has not felt the Psalmist's cry: "Oh that I had wings like a dove! for then would I fly away, and be at rest" (Psa. 55:6). We long for rest, inner peace, and security. Our Father has always supplied these needs. Under the law of Moses, which was civil as well as religious, cities of refuge were designated for those deserving physical protection. Far more important is spiritual refuge.

Every problem of life is basically a spiritual one. Therefore, every solution must have a spiritual base. Our own knowledge is so small, our strength so limited, God's knowledge so limitless, and His love for us so immeasurable, that an earnest desire to please Him becomes the life-goal of all thoughtful people. As expressed in a motto once used by British sailors: "Thy seas are so great, our boats so small."

Heaven's Loving Magnetism

"Yea, I have loved thee with an everlasting love: therefore with loving-kindness have I drawn thee" (Jer. 31:3), said

our Father who "gave his only begotten son" — the ultimate expression of His love. The Son, heaven's magnetic instrument, said:
And I, if I be lifted up from the earth, will draw all men unto me. This he said, signifying what death he should die (Jno. 12:32,33).

This pin-points the pivotal events of all time: Christ's death, resurrection and ascension, which changed the entire course of history, even the way of designating time. Christ is acknowledged each time the date is written. In Him is fulfillment of the promise: "His children shall have a place of refuge" (14:26).

Refuge from Doubt

Nothing is more disquieting than doubt and uncertainty, whether in spiritual knowledge or personal relationships. Our hearts crave absolutes and stability, dependable principles and people, in this world of turmoil and uncertainty.

The Father has provided a fixed and certain Guide, the "Manufacturer's Manual" for the "machine" He created. How consoling! Yet many today are sinking in a spiritual sea of gray, embracing the fallacy that nothing is black or white, right or wrong, nothing true and dependable. Of all books, only the Bible has passed all tests of authenticity. If it is not an infallible Guide, then the Creator placed a miserable assemblage of people on earth to grope through a muddled existence to an uncertain end. An unthinkable and unreasonable conclusion!

So we can confidently affirm, as the apostle Paul: "I KNOW whom I have believed, and am persuaded that he is able to keep that which I have committed unto him against that day" (II Tim. 1:12). There is no need to bear the weight of disquieting doubt, to be "tossed about by every wind of doctrine." We can KNOW that God's word is his counsel, and that "the counsel of the Lord shall stand" (19:21; 21:30).

Refuge from Guilt

The ability to feel guilt is God-given, a spiritual barometer for our protection. Its value should never be minimized, but rightly used. Remorse, regret — these are man's inner verdict against himself, the first necessary step toward improvement. Secular counselors attempt to obliterate guilt by denying its reality. This thwarts guilt's intended benefit, a serious disfavor to those seeking help.

Guilt, realization of wrong-doing, is disquieting and causes fear, not courage. "The wicked flee when no man pursueth" (28:1). Condemned by his own conscience, the sinner tries to escape, but where can he flee for relief? An army chaplain said to a distraught and despondent soldier: "Is there anything I can do for you?" The young man replied: "What I need is for somebody to un-do." Only the Father gives the formula for "un-doing" mistakes.

Refuge from Sin

Sin has gone out of style but not out of practice! The word is seldom used in "enlightened" and "intellectual" circles. And, of course, those who deny the reality of guilt do so because they deny the reality of sin. A number of years ago, as we were participating in a television program, the anchorwoman who was the mother of several teens said: "I have never at any time said the word 'sin' to my children." An unwitting admission that she is not like God, for He uses the word freely and constantly! Sadly, this is not an isolated case. Even many preachers manifest the same attitude. Preachers who try to make people feel comfortable in their sins disgrace their calling, shirk their responsibility, do an injustice to their listeners, and contradict God. Evidently they think if they don't mention sin they can escape the consequences — a naive view which has never worked.

From the beginning until now, human beings have tried to devise their own plans for blotting out sin. Such efforts actually confirm the reality of guilt and sin. Nobody would try to hide something that does not exist! "He that covereth his sins shall not prosper" (28:13). Adam and Eve quickly learned that guilt and sin are very real. They attempted to cover themselves and to hide from God, finding such to be impossible. Their total resource to save themselves was a fig leaf! And man-on-his-own can do no better today.

Sin is reckoned or measured by God, not man; so it must be erased by His instructions, not man's. The Father defines sin. It is either transgression (I Jno. 3:4) or omission (Jas. 4:17) of His law. According to His Word, there are only two things He can do with sin: punish it, or forgive it, which He surely prefers. He is "not willing that any should perish but that all should come to repentance" (II Pet. 3:9).

All of us have sinned (Rom. 3:23) and sin separates us from God (Isa. 59:2). Then how can we be reconciled and reunited with Him? How can we enjoy spiritual refuge?

The Incomparable Invitation

Jesus, heaven's magnet, invites: "Come unto me, all ye that labor and are heavy laden, and I will give you rest. Take my yoke upon you, and learn of me ... and ye shall find rest unto your souls. For my yoke is easy, and my burden is light" (Matt. 11:28-30).

Christians have burdens, but they are light in comparison with the burden of sin. If you are familiar with farm life, you know that a young inexperienced colt is often yoked with an experienced dependable animal. This helps the fretful and rebellious youngster to keep his course, to become a worthy worker. Just think! To learn life's paces, we have the exalted privilege of being yoked with Christ, Wisdom personified. He has been over the road, knows all the pitfalls, and will help bear our burdens. He says:

> *No man can come to me, except the Father which hath sent me draw him: and I will raise him up at the last day. It is written in the prophets, And they shall be all TAUGHT OF GOD. Every man therefore that hath heard, and hath learned of the Father, cometh unto me (Jno. 6:44,45).*

So the magnetism of the Father and the Son draws us, but how? Not mysteriously through the atmosphere. *They shall all be taught.* Only through the Word can we know what the Father and Son have done for us, and what they want us to do. So, to accept Christ's invitation, learning is the first necessary step. "Faith cometh by hearing, and hearing by the word of God" (Rom. 10:17). Only in this way can faith be established in our hearts; and faith is necessary: "Without faith it is impossible to please him: for he that cometh to God must believe that he is, and that he is a rewarder of them that diligently seek him" (Heb. 11:6).

But just believing in God is not sufficient. Christ said: "I am the way, the truth, and the life: no man cometh unto the Father, but by me" (Jno. 14:6). He further says: "For if ye believe not that I am he [the Son of God — deity] ye shall die in your sins" (Jno. 8:24).

Then what is faith? Often we hear the statement: "Just have faith, and everything will be all right." Faith in what? *Faith in faith is indeed a barren creed!* Faith must have an object, a valid one. To understand faith, we must know what it is NOT.

Faith is NOT feeling, NOT something better felt than told. You don't board a plane just because you *feel* it's the right one.

Faith is NOT trying to make yourself believe something in spite of all evidence to the contrary.

Faith is NOT contrary to reason, but based on reason.

Faith IS a valid conclusion based on credible evidence, and faith can be strong enough to equal knowledge. Consider one simple illustration. Suppose someone said to you: "I have two coins in my hand. They equal 35¢. What are they?" Though you couldn't see them, you would KNOW immediately the coins to be a quarter and a dime. Why? That's the only possible answer. It's not contrary to reason or something better felt than told, but a logical conclusion derived from prior knowledge and credible evidence. What you *have seen* bears testimony of what is *not seen*.

An abundance of credible evidence supports an unwavering faith in our Creator, his Son, and his Word. All who doubt or waver should do themselves a favor by thoroughly examining this evidence which can build strong faith. How do we show our faith? By obeying God's commandments, heeding His warnings, and being comforted by His promises. This should be the easiest thing in the world, for the brevity of life should promote trust and obedience. Even the most unlearned knows that he won't be on earth long. "We do all fade as a leaf" (Isa. 64:6).

Be still prepared for death, and life or death shall thereby be the sweeter. — Shakespeare

Incomparable Security

There is only one bomb-proof shelter: abiding in Christ. Fear besets us on all sides: fear of old age, poverty, death, desertion, loneliness, or nuclear war. The vital question is: how can we enter this spiritual shelter? Our faith in Christ as God's Son must prompt repentance of all sins. He said: "Except ye repent, ye shall all likewise perish" (Lk. 13:3). Some mistakenly believe that mere regret over wrong-doing constitutes repentance. Such is necessary, but much more is included. Repentance is a change of heart (mind) which is prompted and preceded by a godly sorrow for sin and followed by a change of conduct. However, this alone is not sufficient. Romans 6:3-6 tells us when and how to be brought into contact with the saving blood of Christ — the blood which blots out sin and makes us a new creature. All who "have been baptized into Christ have put on Christ" (Gal. 3:27). "Therefore, *if any man be in Christ, he is a new creature:* old things are passed away; behold, all things are become new" (II Cor. 5:17).

Those who "put on Christ" become citizens of His kingdom, the kingdom which cannot be shaken or moved. The apostle Paul and other Christians of his day were in that kingdom (Heb. 12:27,28), and we have the same privilege — to live in the place of refuge and spiritual security. As citizens of His kingdom, we must follow Him in all things. "Be thou faithful unto death, and I will give thee a crown of life" (Rev. 2:10). Accepting the incomparable invitation: "Come unto me" involves the incomparable calling and obligation: "Come after me." We now have the glorious privilege of following Christ as our Savior and Guide. Realizing that he will some day be our Judge should prompt willing and grateful obedience (II Cor. 5:10).

Incomparable Riches and Rewards

Suppose someone offered you a treasure more valuable than all the world's silver, gold, or rubies. This is the possibility — an incredible fortune for all who follow the Voice of Wisdom: happiness, peace, pleasantness, honor, and the tree of life (3:13-18). Read also the entire 8th chapter of *Proverbs* and meditate on each promised treasure. Wisdom says: "Riches and honor are with me; yea, durable riches and righteousness" (8:18). These riches include everything needed to fulfill our heart's deepest longings. Living in Christ, who is Wisdom personified, provides every spiritual blessing (Eph. 1:3) — not only freedom from doubt, freedom from guilt, freedom from sin, but also:

Constant companionship — freedom from loneliness. Being

alone is not synonomous with loneliness. One may be loneliest in the midst of a crowd. It is a feeling of isolation, of not belonging, an excruciating pain; but Christ says we need never be lonely. He promises his followers: "Lo, I am with you alway, even unto the end of the world" (Matt. 28:20).

Courage — freedom from fear. Fear besets us on all sides, but those who follow Wisdom can be assured: "The Lord is my helper, and I will not fear what man shall do unto me" (Heb. 13:6). Be comforted by this glorious promise: "When thou liest down, thou shalt not be afraid: yea, thou shalt lie down, and thy sleep shall be sweet. Be not afraid of sudden fear ... the Lord shall be thy confidence" (3:24-26).

Help with burdens too heavy to bear alone. Nothing is more certain than sorrow, problems, and heartaches. Our natural tendency is to shrink back, to avoid trouble at all costs. This is not only impossible but unwise, for adversity is necessary for spiritual growth. Our most valuable lessons are usually learned from our hardest times. What consolation to know that we can be yoked with the Power of the Universe as we pull these heavy loads. How often we overlook one of the richest privileges of all: "Humble yourselves therefore under the mighty hand of God, that he may exalt you in due time: casting all your care upon him; for he careth for you" (I Pet. 5:7).

Many trials and temptations will come. We cannot control the winds. So we must set our sails to bear them, and remember the consoling admonition to cast all our care upon Him because He cares for us.

> I know my heavenly father knows
> The storms that would my way oppose;
> But he can drive the clouds away
> And turn the darkness into day.
> I know my heavenly father knows

And tempers every wind that blows.
—S.M.I. Henry

A feeling of usefulness is necessary for the fulfilled life. We are spiritually restless. Any person who satisfies *every creature comfort* still feels a deep nagging realization that there must be something more to life. Many go through the motions of living, filled with the sense of futility and incompleteness expressed in the popular song: "Is This All There Is?" Every thoughtful person has already learned that life is more than bread and circuses, that "man does not live by bread alone." Following the Voice of Wisdom fills this void and furnishes the only far-reaching purpose for living: keeping our eyes on eternal values and helping others to do so.

Hope is necessary for the good life. Nothing is more devastating than the despair of hopelessness. Hope cannot be plucked out of the air. Hope in hope is a sterile consolation. Hope must have foundation; otherwise, it is a false hope which can never come to fruition. Immortality is taught by Jesus and demonstrated by his resurrection. His message of hope falls upon hearts like showers on a desert. This is the fundamental theme of the Bible. We can, like the patriarch Job, hold to the unchanging in a changing world, hope in the midst of a seemingly hopeless situation. "The righteous have hope in death" (14:32). The tree of life, forfeited in Eden, will be regained in heaven (11:30; Rev. 22:2,14).

Wisdom is to the soul what honey is to the mouth (24:13,14). Then why does not every person avail himself of this sweet and incomparable treasure? Because nothing can make spiritual living palatable to a carnal mind! "They that are after the flesh do mind the things of the flesh" (Rom. 8:5-8). God's ways have no appeal to the person enamoured with the pleasures of sin. Carnal minds are blind to the pleasures of righteousness. If every person could only see how marvelous it is to exchange the pleasures of sin for the pleasures of righteousness! It's like exchanging gaudy tinsel for pure gold. Like exchanging the counterfeit for the real. Like discarding a worn and soiled garment for one of exquisite beauty. It's exchanging confusion for direction, emptiness for fulfillment, famine for feasting, loneliness for companionship, despair for hope.

Indeed, "Riches and honor are with me; yea, durable riches and righteousness." Isn't it thrilling to know that we can *possess* such wealth, and *know* that it cannot be destroyed by inflation, deflation, depression, bankruptcy, wars, tornadoes, fires, floods, death, or anything else the world can hurl at us? Yes, *durable riches!*

FOR THOUGHT OR DISCUSSION

- From the time of Adam and Eve, human beings have tried to devise their own methods of curing the inescapable pain of sin and guilt. All are counterfeit cures, futile and ineffective:

  (1) One effort is to deny sin's existence by re-naming it "sickness," "misbehavior," "maladjustment," or "old-fogey fantasy." Suppose someone should fill a milk carton with cyanide. Would the cyanide's danger be obliterated simply because it's labeled milk? Of course not! The deception would increase the danger. Trying to obliterate sin by re-naming it is the gravest sin of all. It not only assumes a wisdom greater than the Creator, but destroys souls who are unaware of the deception.

  (2) Some try to cover sin by blaming others. "Look what you made me do!" is a common blame-shifting strategy used by children and by some adults. Dangerous self-deception! Each person must account for his own conduct (Rom. 14:12) regardless of what others do.

(3) Sin cannot be nullified by comparing ourselves with others: "I'm not so bad. So-and-so does far worse." Extremely foolish reasoning (II Cor. 10:12). "So-and-so" is not our standard or our Judge.

(4) Others attempt to blot out sin by balancing good and evil, believing that a good deed cancels an evil one. A totally antibiblical idea.

(5) Sin cannot be covered by human philosophies, as previously discussed. A secular psychologist said to a young patient: "Guilt exists only in your mind. Just forgive yourself. Change your own mind, and you will be all right." This popular fallacy promotes a false sense of spiritual security.

(6) Sin cannot be covered simply by the passing of time. Time may dull the sinner's memory and conscience; but if time blotted out sin, there would be absolutely no validity to any part of God's Word.

(7) Sin cannot be covered by a moral life alone. If so, Christ's life and death would have been totally unnecessary and meaningless. Human beings have always had the ability to live morally.

- Then what is the remedy for sin? The necessity of the blood of Christ runs like a crimson thread from Genesis 3:15 through the entire Bible. Limited space forbids a full discussion, but consider some basic principles. The life is in the blood (Lev. 17:11), and "without the shedding of blood there is no remission" (Heb. 9:22). Carefully read the entire 9th chapter of *Hebrews*. Christ said: "For this is the blood of the new testament, which is shed for many for the remission of sins" (Matt. 26:28). His blood is the propitiation (covering) by which our sins can be remitted or forgiven (Rom. 3:24,25). When a believing and penitent person is baptized into Christ (Gal. 3:27; Rom. 6:3-6) then he or she becomes a part of "the church of God which he hath purchased with his own blood" (Acts 20:28).

- Some attempt to embrace Christ's moral teachings while rejecting his deity. An impossible position! Christ claimed to be the Son of God, the only way to the Father. If not, he was the world's chief liar and deceiver — not a good moral man! There is no middle ground.

- Some people chaff at God's law, contending that it's too strict and too confining, a kind of slavery. Not so. Rather, it's liberation, real freedom. Think of a train. It works according to the designer, on track. Yes, narrow and confining from one viewpoint — but the only means of successful operation. As long as he stays on track, the engineer can speed along with assurance and freedom, singing or whistling, benefitting himself and others. However, if the train leaves the narrow confines of the track, the result is tragedy and chaos.

- One of the most heart-stirring of all Scriptures is Abigail's assurance to David that his soul "shall be bound in the bundle of life with the Lord thy God" (I Sam. 25:39). This is also our possibility. As a baby wrapped in a blanket, guarded by loving protective arms, we can be held by our Father, the Creator of the Universe! Security, stability, rest, relief, comfort, warmth, love, concern, protection, and nourishment for our inner being. The Most Magnetic Power draws us and entreats us to enjoy these incomparable riches.

> Never a trial that He is not there;
> Never a burden that He doth not bear;
> Never a sorrow that He doth not share.
> Moment by moment I'm under his care.
>
> Never a heartache, and never a groan,
> Never a tear-drop, and never a moan,
> Never a danger but there, on his throne,
> Moment by moment, He thinks of his own.
> —Daniel W. Whittle

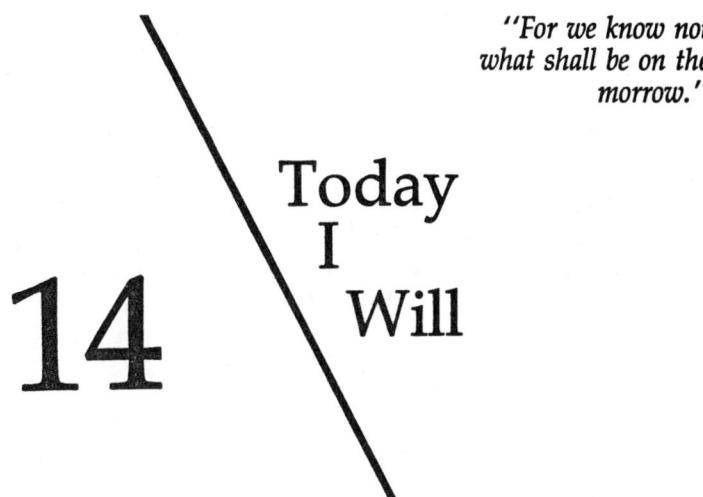

"For we know not what shall be on the morrow."

14 Today I Will

Too often we forget the most obvious truths. We can live only one day at a time. Today is all we have. So choosing life's best must be done *today*. Someone has aptly observed that most of us crucify today between two thieves: yesterday and tomorrow. All of us who have made the good decision to enter God's place of spiritual refuge, to follow Christ at all costs, can resolve that we will each day consciously and deliberately follow the precepts of our Guide, enriching us today and fortifying us for tomorrow. Summarizing principles discussed in previous chapters, let's resolve:

TODAY I WILL thank God for another day of life. Life is so precious. A number of years ago, a soldier was asked: "If you could have any gift in the world, what would it be?" The soldier thoughtfully replied: "Tomorrow." Just to be alive today is such an incomparable blessing that we should never take it for granted and should never neglect to recognize the Giver and Sustainer of all life.

TODAY I WILL observe the wonders of nature as I go about my daily duties. The sky, the birds, the trees, the grass, the flowers, the air we breathe. These cry out to us, begging us to be constantly conscious of a Power greater than any human being, THE POWER in whom "we live, and move, and have our being."

TODAY I WILL rejoice in the exalted privilege of communicating with this Power — as He talks to me through His Word, and I talk to him in prayer. Just imagine! The Creator of the universe. The God of Abraham, Isaac, and Jacob. The Power who holds the whole world in His hands, keeping it from falling apart. And we can simply lift our hearts to Him and talk with Him as a child to his loving Father — anytime, anywhere, under all circumstances, even silently if necessary.

> Speak to him, thou, for he hears,
> And spirit with spirit can meet;
> Closer is he than breathing,
> And nearer than hands and feet.
> —Alfred Tennyson

TODAY I WILL strive to live the prayer of the psalmist: "Let the words of my mouth, and the meditation of my heart, be acceptable in thy sight, O Lord, my strength, and my redeemer" (Psa. 19:14).

TODAY I WILL take time to examine my priorities, remembering that Christ admonishes me: "Seek ye first the kingdom of God, and his righteousness" (Matt. 6:33). What will absorb my mind, my time, my efforts today? Those values which will live in eternity, or things which pass away with this world?

TODAY I WILL be aware that every person I see is a never-dying soul who will spend eternity somewhere. This should prompt me to "think souls" under all circumstances, to be concerned with each person's spiritual welfare.

> God gave me something very sweet to
> be mine own this day;
> A precious opportunity a word
> for Christ to say.

TODAY I WILL remember that time is life. We may be able to save money for the future, but not so with time. As Benjamin Franklin succinctly stated: "Dost thou love life? Then do not squander time, for that's the stuff life's made of." So if you spend one hour with someone today, you have given that person a precious gift, a part of your life which can never be retrieved or replaced.

> The time is short.
> It thou wouldst work for God it must
> be now.
> If thou wouldst win the garlands for
> thy brow,
> Redeem the time.
> I sometimes feel the thread of life
> is slender;
> And soon with me the labor will be
> wrought;
> Then grows my heart to other hearts
> more tender;
> The time is short.

TODAY I WILL remember that God's work is done through Christians. We are His ambassadors, commissioned in heaven to work for awhile in this world of turmoil and sin. If we do not do His work, it will not be done! Not that He lacks power, but His Word clearly identifies His chosen plan. You recall the children's song: "God has no hands but our hands to do his work today." Will I DO HIS WORK TODAY? Some unknown poet prompts a self-examination.

> Somebody did a golden deed;
> Somebody proved a friend in need;
> Somebody sang a beautiful song;
> Somebody smiled the whole day long;
> Somebody thought, " 'Tis sweet to live."
> Somebody said, "I'm glad to give."
> Somebody fought a valiant fight;
> Somebody lived to shield the right;
>   Was that Somebody you?

TODAY I WILL remember that when I allow Christ to be the "other significant Person" in my life — my Friend, Example, Intercessor, and Saviour — there is no way that other human beings can destroy my self-esteem. So TODAY I WILL be comforted by the wonderful promise: "Lo I am with you always, even unto the end of the world."

TODAY I WILL keep in mind that my Saviour has laid upon me the responsibility — and, yes, the glorious privilege — of being LIGHT in this world of spiritual darkness: "Ye are the light of the world." To be *light in the world* requires that we be *different from the world*. If light is *not different from darkness*, then it is not light!

> Brightly beams our Father's mercy
> From his lighthouse evermore;
> But to us He gives the keeping
> Of the lights along the shore.
> —P. P. Bliss

TODAY I WILL speak words of encouragement to lift some weary heart. Most people are fighting uphill battles. Some are on the verge of losing. Everyone needs the sympathetic touch of others, as so plaintively expressed by some unknown writer;

> If I were dead I think that you would come
> And look upon me, cold and white, and say,
> "Poor child! I'm sorry you have gone away."
>
> But just because my body has to live
> Through hopeless years, you do not come and say,
> "Dear child, I'm glad that you are here today."

TODAY I WILL use my hardships and heartaches to promote spiritual growth, remembering that these can draw me closer to the Father, that I may "become partakers of his holiness" (Heb. 12:10), and may also learn thereby to comfort others (II Cor. 1:4).

> I walked a mile with Pleasure;
> She chattered all the way,
> But left me none the wiser
> For all she had to say.
>
> I walked a mile with Sorrow;
> And ne'er a word said she;
> But oh, the things I learned from her
> When Sorrow walked with me!
> —Robert Browning Hamilton

TODAY I WILL strive under all circumstances to put myself in others' place and treat them as I would like to be treated. Christ so instructed in Matthew 7:12, and no wonder it is called the Golden Rule. Its power and importance cannot be over-emphasized. Following this one principle could cure many problems in families, in the church, and in all society. So I will try to look beneath the surface and the trivialities, to be a source of understanding and support to others.

> If I had known what trouble you were bearing;
> What griefs were in the silence of your face;
> I would have been more gentle, and more caring,
> And tried to give you gladness for a space.
> I would have brought more warmth into the place,
> If I had known.
>
> If I had known what thoughts despairing drew you;
> (Why do we never try to understand?)
> I would have lent a little friendship to you,
> And slipped my hand within your hand,
> And made your stay more pleasant in the land,
> If I had known.
> —Mary Carolyn Davies

TODAY I WILL be fortified and encouraged by the assurance that I have a sure and dependable anchor in the midst of life's storms — that I can KNOW God and his Truth — not being tossed about by the many doctrines which assail me daily from every side.

It fortifies my soul to know
That, though I perish, Truth is so;
That, howsoe'er I stray and range,
Whate'er I do, Thou dost not change.
I steadier step when I recall
That, if I slip, Thou dost not fall.
                —Arthur Hugh Clough

TODAY I WILL strive to keep uppermost in my mind these words of Wisdom:

Let us hear the conclusion of the whole matter: Fear God, and keep his commandments: for this is the whole duty of man. For God shall bring every work into judgment, with every secret thing, whether it be good, or whether it be evil.
—*Eccl. 12:13,14*

> Though thy name be spread abroad,
>   Like winged seed, from shore to shore,
> What thou art before thy God,
>   That thou art and nothing more.

TODAY I WILL be comforted, strengthened, and motivated by the incomparably beautiful hope supplied by the promises of the Father and the Son to the faithful ...

... *heirs of God, and joint-heirs with Christ; if so be that we suffer with him, that we may be also glorified together. For I reckon that the sufferings of this present time are not worthy to be compared with the glory which shall be revealed to us* (Rom. 8:17,18).

Let not your heart be troubled: ye believe in God, believe also in me. In my Father's house are many mansions: if it were not so, I would have told you. I go to prepare a place for you. And if I go and prepare a place for you, I will come again, and receive you unto myself; that where I am, there ye may be also (Jno. 14:1-3).

* * * *

And God shall wipe away all tears from their eyes; and there shall be no more death, neither sorrow, nor crying, neither shall there be any more pain: for the former things are passed away (Rev. 21:4).

* * * *

>Only today is mine,
> And that I owe to Thee;
>Help me to make it thine;
> As pure as it may be;
>Let it see something done,
>Let it see something won,
>Then at the setting sun
> I'll give it back to thee.
>
>What if I cannot tell
> The cares the day may bring?
>I know that I shall dwell
> Beneath Thy sheltering wing;
>And there the load is light;
>And there the dark is bright,
>And weakness turns to might,
> And so I trust and sing.
>
>   —Henry Burton